This book is dedicated to six gallant
and honourable officers:

The Reverend Major General Morgan Llewellyn, *Royal Welsh Fusiliers*
Brigadier C. J. Lee, *South Wales Borderers*
Major Tim Wakefield, *The Welsh Guards*
Pilot Officer Mike Chappell
Lt Col Richard Parry, *Queens Dragoon Guards*
Also to the late Sir Tasker Watkins VC, *Welch Regiment*

The author would like to thank the following for their support and sponsorship during the writing and preparation of this book:

The Laura Ashley Foundation
Dr John and William Gibbs and their Trust.
Richard Griffiths
William Powell. A.M.
Trevor Rodwell
Chris Thomas
Roger Williams M.P.
The Regimental Museum of The Royal Welsh
Jonathan Fonseca
Richard and Rhos Wyatt

Also to Alun Jones for proof reading this book, Jan Morris for writing the prologue, Professor the Rev. D. P. Davies for the review, Frances Chaffey for all her help and invaluable secretarial work and, of course, Robert Macdonald for his illustrations.

The author and publisher acknowledge the kind copyright permission granted by the following:

Barbara Levy Literary Agency (Siegfried Sassoon)
Siwan (Saunders Lewis)
Robin Llywelyn (Clough William-Ellis)
David Higham Literary, film and T.V. agents
(Dylan Thomas and Anthony Powell)
David Raikes (David Raikes)
Sioned O'Connor (Cynan)
John Ottewell

At the end of each essay one or more books are mentioned as a suggestion for further reading.

ISBN 978-0-9930268-0-5

CONTENTS

REVIEW BY D. P. DAVIES
Professor Emeritus of Theology, University of Wales.

Critics sometimes maintain that a work of art or a literary composition such as a poem can be appreciated for its own sake, irrespective of the identity of the artist or poet or the circumstances of its creation. This study of Welsh War Poets takes the opposite view. Jonathan Morgan seeks to show that the creative work of a series of artists/poets can be better understood if we take full account of their Welshness (or lack of it), their spirituality (or lack of it) and, above all in this context, their reaction to being plunged into the horrors of war.

In particular, the author (to a large extent, as he himself admits, for personal reasons derived from his own experience of being Welsh, having served in action in the Army, being deeply interested in things spiritual and especially having suffered for many years from post-traumatic stress) wishes to explore how the lives and work of his chosen subjects have been shaped by and therefore reflect their attitudes to being Welsh or related to Wales, their spiritual journeys and attempts to make sense of the horrors of warfare, their inter-relationships with fellow soldiers and how they dealt with post-traumatic stress.

Following a brief introduction Morgan looks at twenty-one examples of 'Welsh poets' (or twenty three if we add as individuals those who are in pairs - Frank Richards and Llywelyn Wyn Jones, on the one hand, and Augustus and Gwen John, on the other). The book ends with an extended personal reflection on his own life and experience by the author himself and some interesting and moving examples of his own poetry.

The first poet to be introduced is Henry Vaughan, the only representative of pre-twentieth century times. Certainly his poetry deserves the attention of critics of any age, but he sits rather oddly alongside those whose experience was profoundly different. The bulk of the 'poets' (appropriately given that this year marks the centenary of the outbreak) are from the period of the

First World War. Morgan introduces us to fourteen individual artists/poets in all (four of them in pairs, as noted above). Some are indisputably Welsh (Cynan, Hedd Wyn and Saunders Lewis) in that their work was largely, even exclusively, written in Welsh. Others are less identifiably Welsh – Siegfried Sassoon, for example, is not a poet normally associated with Wales or the Welsh. Not all are poets in the narrow sense – Clough Williams Ellis was primarily an architect, David Jones was in main an artist, as were Augustus John and his sister, Gwen. In my view, the inclusion of such artists enhances the book and widens its scope in a fruitful way. Morgan might perhaps have focused even more on the way each individual reacted to the trauma of war, since this seems to be the most distinctive element in his thesis. He certainly succeeds in showing that those most directly involved were not in any way disposed to glory in battle, but rather were concerned to show how horrific, futile even, armed conflict really is.

The list of World War Two artists/poets/writers is fewer – eight in all. Some are very well known names – Raymond Williams and Rex Whistler, for example. Others are less well-known, so it is good to have included David Raikes and John Ottewell for example. Eyebrows may be raised at the inclusion of Dylan Thomas, notwithstanding his popularity and quality of his poetry. To have him as a 'war poet' is, to my view, a case of special pleading. Or is he included as a kind of anti-hero?

This is an interesting and informative collection of short essays.

PROLOGUE
by Jan Morris

At the failure of his battles against the British in Egypt in 1882, the imprisoned Egyptian nationalist Ahmed Orabi, known to his enemies as Arabi Pasha, was sentenced to death, but wrote these words to his Welsh gaoler, Major Baldwin Evans of Rhuddlan:

'My good and honourable friend, Mr Evans, I beg to offer you my devotion for the great zeal and trouble you have taken on our behalf during your frequent visits to us in our prison cell. I pray God to reward you for your great kindness to us in our hours of grief and darkness.'

I know nothing more about Major Evans, but I have long honoured his memory, and he seems to me to offer a proper introduction to this book. He was evidently a Welsh soldier with a compassionate heart, and 'The Tragedy of War' concerns itself with twenty other Welshmen who, caught up in one way or another with military miseries and demands, responded as Major Evans did.

As it happens, they were all artistic people, many of them remembered chiefly for their creative gifts but Jonathan Morgan treats them fundamentally as comrades. He has been a soldier himself, invalided out of the Royal Regiment of Wales after a cruel tour of duty in Ireland and many of his characters themselves served in one or other of the Welsh regiments of the British Army, nowadays consolidated into the Royal Welsh. He likes to think that his unit has an artistic tradition 'probably greater than any other regiment of the British Army,' and it is his purpose to show us how often spiritual feeling has informed, softened and inspired the relationships of Welsh artists with the harsh realities of militarism.

Some of his chosen characters, one has to say, are more Welsh than others (Robert Graves was half Irish and half German) and some had no more than a tangential experience of war (Dylan Thomas was most certainly never on parade). Morgan is concerned, though, to show us how the Welsh artistic sensibility has responded to the realities of armed conflict, whether in the abstract or actually on the field of battle - seven of his characters were killed in action.

His roster has its surprises. Who would have thought that Henry Vaughan, the divine metaphysician of Llansantffraid, had ever been a soldier? Or that Lawrence of Arabia was born at Tremadog? Or that Clough Williams-Ellis of Portmeirion had fought in the first great tank battle, at Cambrai in 1917 and written the first history of the weapon? He has enlisted them all though because he believes their responses to war have been affected by their association with Cymreictod, Welshness - the tremulous, fragile, sometimes ambiguous abstraction that has sustained the nation down the centuries.

Morgan believes that near the heart of that loyalty lies a profound compassion, expressed in the words and music of Welsh artists down the ages. So do I, but since there is to Welshness a proud military tradition too, I think it proper that this book should commemorate all the Hedd Wynns, all the Wilfred Owens, all the Alun Lewises - yes, and all the long-forgotten Baldwin Evanses - who have tempered our soldiering history with kindness and regret.

INTRODUCTION

It gives me huge pleasure to introduce these wonderful artists in the full meaning of the word. Some of them need no introductions. However, I thought I would look at them in a slightly different way from that in which they are usually treated. Firstly, I will look at how they perceived their Welshness. Secondly, I will try to look at the spirituality behind their work. Thirdly, I will examine how they got on with their fellow officers and men and lastly, how they dealt with post traumatic stress. Not all were in the great infantry regiments of Wales, the Welsh Guards, the Royal Welch Fusiliers, the South Wales Borderers and the Welsh Regiment but many were. The new regiment, the Royal Welsh, which has been formed out of three of these regiments inherits an artistic tradition probably greater than any other regiment in the British Army. This was partly due to the creative nature of the Celts and to the nature of the regiments, especially the Royal Welch Fusiliers. The Welsh Guards were the latest to be formed; in the officers' mess in peacetime they were known as the Foreign Legion as many of their officers were not Welsh. Rex Whistler was typical, although he had close links with the Angleseys. Clough Williams-Ellis was an example of a Welshman in the Welsh Guards. Rex Whistler was typical, although he had close links with the Angleseys. Clough Williams-Ellis was an example of a Welshman in the Welsh Guards and, of course, many more joined in wartime. The Royal Welch Fusiliers, certainly in my day, were very comfortable in their Welshness. They had been founded by a Welshman, the Lord Herbert, and they were very relaxed with the men and the officers coming from Wales and getting on well together as a team. Even to this day, with names like Kyffin Williams and General Morgan Llewellyn, their culture lives on. The Borderers were a different kettle of fish. For a long time they had been the 24th Regiment of Foot raised in Kent by Sir Edward Dering; only latterly had they come to the Border country and then, perceiving that the Norman lords were very hard on the Welsh, seemed to adopt a 'white or English' officer mentality. Although the author personally did not serve in the S.W. Borderers, his godfather did and won the MC. When they joined with the Welch Regiment, which by this time had become a good old middle-class Welsh regiment in the officers' mess, they tended to patronise the latter. This was partly because they felt they had a superior brand name after the great film depicting the Zulu wars. They felt it was important in the officers' mess to have a distance between the officers and the men and therefore recruited English public schoolboys to the mess who often had no affinity with Wales.

This culture led to a number of unsavoury incidents in the author's early years as a young officer. Firstly, he was taken out by two young non-Welsh captains and told he should never expect to get anywhere as a Welshman in the Royal Regiment of Wales. Secondly, a non-Welsh officer described him as having the features of a miner as if it were some sort of insult. Thirdly, one English public schoolboy described the men as 'pond life'. Also the adjutant, in his time, talked about white or English officers in a Welsh regiment as if thousands of Welsh officers had not died for their country.

There had always been a clever manipulation of the Celts in the armed forces based on a perceived inferiority complex. This is the background to many of our heroes in this book – Saunders Lewis for example was never feted by the SWB because of his Welsh Nationalism despite his bravery in the First World War. Alun Lewis, probably the greatest poet of the Second World War, was treated likewise because he was thought to have committed suicide. The Welsh have not always had a good time in the British Army; for instance Kitchener, at one time the chief of Imperial Staff, was rather disparaging about Welsh senior officers, partly because he disliked Lloyd George's interference in his appointments.

The author has personal experience of this, having been invalided out with post traumatic stress partly brought about by a collapse of confidence in his own Welshness. He also had a dreadful tour of Northern Ireland in 1972. The author has great empathy with these wonderful artists he writes about who often hated war and were saddened by it.

It has been said in the past that the Welsh are some of the greatest defensive troops in the world. They can be very stubborn and bloody-minded but, if things are explained to them reasonably, they will follow their officers anywhere, so long as they care about and try to understand them. They are great soldiers, courageous and loyal and it was the author's great privilege to be one of their officers. It would be too long here to go through every poet, artist and writer who has been written about. The major themes have been discussed and the wars covered start with Henry Vaughan and the Civil War up until people like Raymond Williams in the Second World War. One of their common traits was that they were communicators and communicate so well the tragedy and hopelessness of war.

Most of them were very brave although some of them, like Dylan Thomas, did not take part in fighting. Most were decent men caught up in the terrible storm of war and tried to cope with it in the best way they could, despite their imagination and Celtic sensibilities.

Wales had made a huge contribution to the war effort. More men proportionately had joined the colours than those from other parts of the British Isles. It is estimated that between 1914 and 1918 some 273,000 men were recruited either as volunteers or as conscripts to serve in the army. 250,000 served in one of the Welsh regiments and around 185,000 served overseas at some point. 40,000 of these died, mainly in Western Europe.

'Wales at War, Critical Essays on Literature and Art' edited by Tony Curtis
'Out of the Fire of Hell', Welsh Experience of the Great War 1914-18 in prose and verse' edited by Alan Llwyd
'After the First Death, an Anthology of Wales and War in the Twentieth Century' edited by Tony Curtis
'Wales on the Western Front' edited by John Richards
'The Red Sweet Wine of Youth, the Brave and Brief Lives of the War Poets' by Nicholas Murray

POST TRAUMATIC STRESS

Mind doctors, i.e. psychiatrists, neurologists and psychologists, came to the field of battle mainly in the 20th century, and they are often known by the troops as shrinks, trick cyclists and nut pickers. The aftermath of war was an extreme environment for them where they could study the shattered mind. They were often asked to cure and send the psychological casualties back to battle, but many felt guilty doing this.

As time went on, many characteristics of the men were said to contribute to their fighting ability; heredity, upbringing, the society they came from, how they felt about the war, and what they felt about their fellow soldiers. Some felt they had to be cruel to be kind. Some felt the soldiers ought to 'get it off their chest' rather than to bottle it up. After the First World War, only the Australians really published an adequate history of shell shock. For a long time, the analysis of these psychological problems was rudimentary, and it was not really until the 1980's that Vietnam was a catalyst to rediscovery and heightened learning on military psychiatry.

As we shall see in this book, Dr William Rivers was a humane and sympathetic figure, who dismissed some of the more heinous methods of electrical torture. Rivers, though, it has often been argued, was better with officers than other ranks. The term 'post traumatic stress disorder' was created by the American Psychiatric Association in 1980. Dr Paul Davis in 1945 talked about those who had broken down, especially of the shame they experienced. There was a large movement in America to help the Vietnam veterans, although some people would say that the treatment turned them into chronic cases. There has always been a clash between the tough and tender approaches, and the realist tradition became unfashionable and was replaced by studies that were more influenced by the drama and emotions caused by the battlefield. The Falklands proved a big learning curve for the establishment in Britain. The Ministry of Defence denied that there was such a problem. Even in 1990, a British Army officer saw PTS as a weakness of character. The Welsh Guards were a case in point, especially after the bombing of the Sir Galahad. In 1987, two army doctors did a study of 64 veterans still serving in the British Army; half of them were reported to have symptoms of PTSD. 22% of them were rated as having the complete syndrome. Many critics claim that about one in five Falklands veterans were suffering from nightmares, depression, alcohol or drug abuse and other mental disorders. Many found the transition from the horrors of the battlefield to the ordinary daily living of home life too difficult an adjustment. In the Gulf War, Gulf War Syndrome was experienced by many troops, and thought to be caused by the enriched uranium shells, vaccines against chemical and bacterial weapons and organophosphate chemicals. One of the results of the study of illness that affects the brain, immune system, cardiovascular system and hormonal responses was that it was known to be caused by stress and the fearful anticipation of war. There is no doubt, going back to the Welsh Guards and their traumatic experience on the Sir Galahad, that, previously, much was made of the inadequacy of their training leading up to the Falklands. Coming from palace duties they were criticised but as a regiment went on to perform so magnificently in Afghanistan, it was obvious that the regiment had few lasting problems.

There was a survey commissioned by Congress in 1983, reported in 1988, that fifteen years after the last American combatant had left Vietnam, 479,000 of the 3.14 million men who served there still had PSD. There was a great chorus after this, which claimed that the whole industry around PSD had turned many veterans into dependent welfare junkies. There was also some criticism of the Outreach programme for Veterans and the Vet Centres created in 1979, which were said to encourage veterans to feed off each other. The centres were based on a hope that mass treatment would be the best way forward. A huge shift in values has taken place in society, and some psychiatrists would say that some men today are incapable of fighting war without psychological damage.

From the author's point of view, when he was invalided out with psychiatric difficulties, it was partly caused by in-fighting in the regiment, a terrible tour of Ireland in 1972, and being brought up on the edge of the 1960s 'hippie' culture; a combination which was enough to turn anyone's brain. His treatment in Woolwich was perfunctory, with very little counselling, and after his father's intervention, a war hero himself, he was abandoned on the streets of London with very little back up. A plethora of military charities has not helped his focus on aid from the military, as he believes this has confused many other veterans. Bringing all the charities together into one major organisation would clarify the situation enormously.

There is one area where the military may have fallen down, and that is where many spirits have been broken by war, a dry, mechanical medicine has tried to heal where spiritual healing would help. Here, we should record the author's father's citation from Squadron Leader C. A .Room (RAF) in which he says, 'On behalf of my colleagues, all ex prisoners of war, I am anxious to trace the widow of our former and well beloved chaplain in 3 prison camps. He was with us when 800 RAF prisoners were transported in a rusty, decrepit hulk of a merchant ship from Memel in Lithuania, through the Baltic to Stetin, confined in a cellar half full of coal dust and fed only with the bare minimum of food and water for 3 days. Arriving at Gross Tychow in Poland we were subjected to the infamous 'run up the road' where SS and Marines directed by a deranged Nazi captain, stabbed and beat the prisoners at will and set brutal dogs on them as they were forced to run the 5 kilometres to the camp. Six months later in February 1944, with the Russian onslaught approaching, we were sent out on a death march of 600 miles across Poland and deep into Germany. We existed on what we could gather from the fields or steal from the various barns and farms where we were billeted nightly. The freezing weather, the lack of food, and the arduous conditions of the march took its toll,and almost 200 of the original 800 did not survive. During this march, Padre Morgan and the three camp doctors (RAMC) performed heroics for those who suffered. Those of us who still survive and meet and correspond regularly will never forget them or their devotion and dedication.'

The author was in Belize when his nerve went and there was no padre to help. It is interesting that a friend of the author, the Welsh poet Owen

Shears, has written a play, 'The Two Worlds of Charlie F', where he brings together many injured service men to perform and express their anger. Robert Ardrey in his great book 'The Territorial Imperative' discusses aggression and there is no doubt that even after the Empire had come to an end, Britain thought that it had a tried and tested formula for controlling territory. Aggression leads to fighting and it is almost an inevitable part of man's nature although many of us, particularly those of us veterans who have seen war, long for peace. It is only a minority who revel in war, but we do need an army to protect our freedom and perhaps we even need nuclear weapons to defend us against the power of irrational and brutal states and their leaders who might have ambitious and greedy temptations to take our relatively wealthy territory and destroy our freedom. In a relatively free and democratic country, war must always be a last resort and those veterans injured by it should be looked after and appreciated, not left on the streets and forgotten. The Army must be an honourable institution, not one divided by in fighting and Darwinian competition.

THE ORIGINS OF THE WELSH REGIMENTS

Since the time of King Arthur, the Welsh military have had a mystique about them. They came out of the mists at the Romans, often successfully, and it took William the Conqueror one day to beat Harold's Anglo Saxon Army and the Normans at least 400 years partially to subdue the Welsh. Edward I took many Welsh archers with him on his march to Scotland. In the time of the 100 Years War, Edward III's armies were full of Welshmen owing allegiance to his son, the Black Prince. They had a roughness and esprit de corps peculiar to themselves. English speakers were deliberately excluded from ranks. They were among the first soldiers on either side to wear full uniform: the green and white of the Black Prince's men from the North, the red and white of the Earl of Arundel's men from Churchland. They marched with their local leaders behind their own leaders. On the marches, the Welsh marched and in many cases proved to have more stamina than the English who rode. They brought their own chaplains and physicians and interpreters. Their archers were renowned at such battles as Crecy.

Henry V hardly recruited from North Wales as he didn't trust former Glyndwr loyalists, but many of his archers came from South Wales; there were about 500 at Agincourt: Roger Vaughan, Watkin Lloyd and Dafydd Gam all helped to rescue the King at one stage in the battle; it is said they were all knighted for their bravery. They had led a contingent of 160 archers from Brecon and district which had mustered at Tretower before joining the march.

Dafydd Gam had been hostile to Owain Glyndwr and was represented as Fluellen by Shakespeare. Even at this time, leeks represented Wales as an emblem after a battle with the Anglo Saxons had resulted in the Welsh tying leeks to their helmets to distinguish themselves. It is interesting that green and white were for long the royal colours of Wales, and it was only when Lloyd George found the raw leek indigestible that St Peter's Leek, the daffodil, was chosen as a more respectable emblem. The Welsh Guards, to this day, wear a leek on their badge. Henry Tudor's march from Dale to Bosworth brought together, especially when the Stanleys came in on his side, a mainly Welsh army against a mainly English one Henry carried, as one of his main standards, the red dragon of Cadwallader on a background of green and white. The Tudors were an old Anglesey family and Henry had been born in Pembroke Castle and brought up as a ward of the Herberts in Raglan Castle for the thirteen years of his life. He might even have learnt some Welsh.

His great ally, Sir Rhys ap Thomas from Carmarthen, who brought him much of the bulk of his army, probably slew Richard III in the battle. The Tudors coming to the throne brought to prominence Henry's personal bodyguard, which became the Yeoman of the Guard on which there was more than a smattering of Welsh representation. They could be described as the oldest regiment in the Army. It is interesting that David Cecil, who founded that great family, went along with Henry Tudor and probably was a Yeoman of the Guard. The author told the Prince of Wales that Oliver Cromwell's real name was Oliver Morgan Williams, the family being a Welsh brewing family who moved up to Cambridgeshire and then adopted the powerful maternal uncle, Thomas Cromwell's name. Wales was split in the civil war but Cromwell's influence pervaded the New Model Army.

In the Napoleonic Wars, the author was told, there was a plaque in one of the great South Coast Towns, saying there were 160 Welsh seamen at the Battle of Trafalgar. It was not then until 1689, under the direction of Lord Herbert of Cherbury, that the RWF were formed. The South Wales Borderers were formed from the Warwickshires in 1881 and were not called that name in the Zulu Wars although they did recruit from Brecon. The Welch or the 41st Regiment were formed in 1881 out of the 69th and 41st Regiment of Foot. In the First World War more Welshmen were recruited proportionately than men from any other part of the British Isles, approximately 280,000, about 25% of the population of men who were called up. The Welsh Guards were formed at the behest of Lloyd George, although the RWF turned down the offer to turn themselves into a Guards regiment. Only one division of Welshmen was formed, although Lloyd George wanted an Army corps, generals of Welsh stock were not common but significant ones were Picton at Waterloo, who rode into battle in a frock coat, and Major General Lewis Pugh Evans VC from Cardiganshire who commanded the Black Watch. General Sir Hugh Rowlands VC, was the commandant of the Transvaal in the Boer War and was instrumental in the setting up of the first concentration camps. There were a number of generals in the First and Second World Wars, some in Burma. Admiral Evan Thomas was deputy commander at the Battle of Jutland.

The Welsh have always been a fighting race, but everyone loves a winner; although we all respect Prince Llywelyn and Owain Glyndwr, it was the archers of the 100 Years War and Henry Tudor who won. The one regiment we haven't really mentioned is the Queen's Dragoon Guards, which came out of the KDG and Bays in 1959. They evolved into the Welsh Cavalry Regiment and were involved in the first Gulf War and the Second Gulf War, and have also done a number of tours of Afghanistan. They are a very fine regiment, and have become Wales's very own cavalry regiment. Welsh officers the author knew were Brigadier Georgie Powell, Lt Col Richard Parry and Mike Richards.

HENRY VAUGHAN

VAUGHAN'S pedigree was impressive, being related to Sir Roger Vaughan who commanded bands of the Welsh archers at Agincourt; also to the Herberts of Raglan and the Somersets. Henry, in writing to one of the Aubreys in later life, says, "My brother and I were born at Newton in the parish of St Bridgets in the year 1621." Not a stone remains in its original place in the present house of Newton which is situated between Scethrog and Llansantffraed under the wooded hillside of Allt-yr-Esgair. Vaughan, in many ways, was a home bird who needed his roots. He felt inspired by the mythology and magic of Wales. Religiously, their background was devoutly Christian and Anglican. At a relatively early age Henry went up to Jesus College, Oxford, which was full of Welshmen. It had been founded by Dr Hugh Price, a Brecon butcher's son, at the behest of Elizabeth 1. Henry is not recorded as matriculating but probably used it as a sort of finishing school from whence to go on to study law in London. On arriving in London, he had entered the Parliamentary lions' den. With the outbreak of the Civil War the King had moved his court to Oxford. In the May Day riots of 1640 before the outbreak of war, great crowds gathered, demonstrating against the hated Archbishop Laud. He spent some time in the taverns sampling the atmosphere of wildness and some elegance. His twin brother, Thomas, was committed to the King's side. In 'Misery', one of his poems at the time, he talks about the age, 'The present times are not to snudge in and embrace a cot. Action and blood now get the game, I'd loose those knots thine hands did tie then would go travel, fight or die.' His brother, William, died of war wounds in 1648. Henry Vaughan had himself gone to war against the Roundheads in 1645. It is not surprising that Vaughan's vocabulary was often one of war. There seems to be a perpetual obsession with blood, bows and glory. Henry was appalled at the Cavalier defeat. He talks about his world being subject to vast movements of violence. His elegy on Mr R W, killed at the Battle of Rowten Heath in 1645 and that on Mr R Hall, killed at Pontefract in 1648, talk about the Cavalier martyr 'As some star hurled in diurnal motions from afar'. In Brecon, Colonel Herbert Price had been the governor of Brecon Castle and MP for the town; he headed the Vaughans' regiment at Chester. In April 1644 Price raised troops for the King in Brecon and, the following summer, entertained King Charles at the Priory. It is possible that Vaughan could have met him there for this is where Vaughan had done much of his courting of Catherine Wise. The King certainly made a great impression on Vaughan who was anguished at Charles's death. There is not a lot of evidence of Vaughan's military service, although in the poem, 'Upon a cloak lent him by Mr J Ridsley', he talks about the adventures of a rough cloak and shows himself as a soldier present at the rough siege of Chester.

It is probable he was at the Battle of Rowten Heath which marked the defeat of the Cavaliers and the King was forced to retreat to Chester. However, after the battle itself, the remnant of the Royalist army retreated to Beeston Castle upon whose surrender in 1645 the defeated Cavaliers were allowed to march across the Dee into Denbigh. Meanwhile, the inhabitants had pulled down their town walls to prevent devastation and had eventually welcomed the Parliamentary troops. It was downhill all the way for Henry and his family. Their devotion to the King's cause made them outcasts in their own world and, although it is probable Henry accepted the sufferings and roughness of war because of his devotion to the Royalist cause, later he became much more of a pacifist in his outlook which was more acceptable to his mysticism and peaceful poetry in the Usk valley. The War was a huge upheaval after his childhood in gentle gentrified Breconshire and brought him face to face with the realities of death and ruthless politics. Civil war is never easy for any country and Henry's life was moulded by its reality and by the defeat of High Anglicanism and the descent into fundamental Puritanism. The latter went against the temperament and instinct of Henry Vaughan who, although always a Welshman, felt he had to take sides in a conflict that turned his fellow countrymen against one another. There is not a lot of war poetry in his writing but, what exists is concerned with heroism and the rightness of the King's cause. There is also not much evidence of his relationship with his fellow soldiers but his mind and spirit were not destroyed by cynicism and bitterness because his poetry, with its great themes of God and Wonder and the Supernatural, continued to be created long after the War. One of the great metaphysical poets from Wales, like his cousin George Herbert who represented the Celtic affinity with the supernatural, he was born a Welshman, lived in Wales most of his life and his destiny was tied up with the cruel times he lived in.

Siegried Sassoon's poem , 'On the Grave of Henry Vaughan' sums him up and reads as follows:

'Above the voiceful windings of a river
An old green slab of simply graven stone
Shuns notice, overshadowed by a yew.
Here Vaughan lies dead, whose name flows on for ever
Through pastures of the spirit washed with dew
And starlit with eternities unknown.
Here sleeps the Silurist; the loved physician;
The face that left no portraiture behind;
The skull that housed white angels and had vision
Of daybreak through the gateways of the mind.
> *Here faith and mercy, wisdom and humility*
> *(Whose influence shall prevail for evermore)*
> *Shine. And this lowly grave tells Heaven's tranquillity*
> *And here stand I, a suppliant at the door.'*

'Henry Vaughan: The Complete Poems' edited by Alan Rudrum

CLOUGH WILLIAMS ELLIS
25 MAY, 1883

CLOUGH'S father was John Clough Williams Ellis M.A, J.P. who was for twenty years fellow and tutor of Sidney Sussex College, Cambridge, and for ten years rector of Gayton, Monmouthshire before he retired to Glasfryn near the small village of Llangybie in the region above Criccieth and Chwelog in Caernarfonshire. Mabel, his mother, was from a Birmingham family who had invested in the slate quarry in Blaenau Ffestiniog, the source of the family's wealth. John and Mabel had four surviving sons of which Clough was the second. Clough was born in Gayton on 25th May 1883. It is interesting that although Clough was brought up in this devout family he was never pious and was particularly a rationalist in outlook. As a boy he was accident-prone but his 'easy come, easy go' style of upbringing brought about especially by his mother was one based on common sense and freedom.

On his father's retirement to Glasfryn, he encountered a rather bleak country area but Clough took to country pursuits and, in particular, he enjoyed hunting. Clough was quite proud of his lineage; his paternal grandmother, for instance, was descended from Sir Richard Clough of Plas Clough in the Vale of Clwyd, who had been Queen Elizabeth's agent in the Netherlands. The Williams side also is said to have been around in the sixteenth century living in Plas Bronderw.

His early education was conducted by a governess and, from the start, he had a healthy disregard of religiosity. He was extremely proud of his Welsh ancestry but had little in common with the local boys as he spoke only very poor Welsh. Despite his Victorian upbringing he was essentially a free spirit. He became a man of independence and self-reliance; he was very much his own man, and the roots of this were created in his boyhood. One of the things he was concerned about was outward appearance and style and he often disapproved of those who fell short on both counts.

He was, in his teens, beginning to be fascinated by architecture and the shape of buildings, although grand ones were few and far between in the area. Tanrallt, his Aunt Hilda's residence, was one of his favourites and they got on extremely well. At fourteen he was dispatched to a famous public school in Northamptonshire called Oundle. His headmaster, Frederick Sanderson, was a man of liberal views against the established and pervading ethos of late Victorian times.

Clough saw in Sanderson and especially his science lessons a fellow traveller and although he was unhappy with much of Oundle, he seemed to have engaged its headmaster. He spent much of his time trying to get out of the school environs, which is why he formed the photographic society and even joined the choir for its outings. He ended up a bit of a philistine, certainly in academic terms, achieving only one per cent in his final French exam.

One of his most lasting impressions of the Oundle area was the Elizabethan ruin of Kirby Hall, which he adored and was quite lyrical about in later years. Sometime during his latter years at Oundle he passed on a tram through the smoke and slums of London's East End; this again was to leave an abiding impression on him against bad architecture. He left Oundle in 1900. He dabbled in architecture for a time before becoming involved in it full time, although not fully qualified.

Clough was 32 when the First World War broke out. He was virtually dismissed as too old for recruitment but he persevered, feeling it his duty to enlist. At the start he was enlisted into the Imperial Light Horse which mutated into a battalion of the Royal Fusiliers. Meantime, he had become engaged to Miss Strachey, daughter of St. Lowe Strachey, editor and proprietor of the 'Spectator'. He then heard that the Welsh Guards had formed and he joined them at Sandown Racecourse. For a wedding present from his fellow officers he asked them for money for a ruin, which was eventually rebuilt on a hill top behind Brondanw. The honeymoon was allowed to last for only four days before Clough was dispatched to the front line. He found himself in the Hohenzollern redoubt. Confusion was at its worst and he had to take over from his company commander. The war was sheer horror for him; he wrote later, 'I seem all through to have contrived to take a curiously detached view of the whole war as far as my part in it went and to have disclaimed responsibility for it or its conduct or its conclusion and generally to have reserved the right to have remained fatalistically critical.' He experienced some of the terrible tedium of routine trench warfare and spent a lot of time doing water-colours and sketches.

He would spend a lot of time, when he could, exploring the local area and even the Prince of Wales, attached to the Guards division headquarters, lent him a horse. His sketching was noticed and he was taken off routine trench duties to survey and sketch enemy positions. Afterwards he tended to joke a lot about his own experience and he was very amused when the army allowed him to survey in an aeroplane. His new occupation did have a few perks such as much greater opportunity to rove around the countryside. He also began to collect various architectural items which he stored in the headquarters cellar. This survey and landscaping work meant he had to do quite a lot of desk work. However Clough realised how terrible it was for the troops in the front line. He also began to get ideas that Britain, when the troops returned, should be a land fit for heroes and the best of it conserved.

He became interested in tanks and, through his usual persistence, got a transfer to the third tank brigade just before the Battle of Arras. His senior officer was Major Boots Hotblack who was severely wounded in a skirmish and Clough had to take over command. The tanks swept forward in the the great battle of Cambrai and then on to victory. It was in recognition of his courage in tank warfare that Clough was awarded a Military Cross. He wrote a book on the history of the tank corps which became a standard reference and he was one of the first to perceive the importance of tanks in the new warfare. When later he came to think about the war he also, like Sassoon and Owen, leant towards pacifism. The sheer scale of modern warfare appalled him, 'The fabulous destruction of life, wealth and beauty'. He goes on to say, 'War is the most disastrous madness for all concerned and my abhorrence of it inevitably led me to take an interest and even some small part in politics. Incidentally, it left me greatly questioning much that in the old days I had innocently accepted as right or at any rate inevitable.'

There is no doubt that Clough was a man of sensitivity, that he perceived the beauty of the countryside and that, although disillusioned somewhat by the industrialisation of Britain and being a bit of a loner, he did appreciate the positive virtues in his fellow man. He took to the war with the panache and courage expected of a Guards officer and of one of his family background but he never embraced it and, always at the back of his mind, there was the feeling that it was totally negative and destructive and should be avoided at all costs. He went on to be one of the great men of Wales, preserving its countryside and adding one of its jewels in Portmeirion, a colourful village of great architectural variety. Like so many of our artists his character was forged in that terrible war and, although he came out unscathed, he never forgot the awful experience and what it did to people. He died in 1978 having again like many of our survivors lived life to the full.

'Clough Williams Ellis, the Architect of Portmeirion, Memoir' by Jonah Jones

WILFRED OWEN

O NE of the purposes of this book is to look at the origins of our poets, especially if they were Welsh. The Owens, as a family, were rather ambivalent about their Welsh origins, mainly because both sides of the family had lived in Nantwich in Cheshire for a number of generations.

However, part of the family mythology was that the Owens were descended from one Baron Lewis Owen, a famous sheriff of Merionethshire in Tudor times. The ambivalence was amplified when Wilfred was described as a Welsh poet in a 1944 radio broadcast. His sister wrote to The Listener to say that 'We are an English family. Wilfred would I am sure have mildly refuted the suggestion that he was Welsh'. This letter was actually written for her by Wilfred's brother, Harold, who swung between being happy to claim Welsh descent and perhaps finding it a bit down market.

There is no doubt that Wilfred hoped to get himself attached to a Welsh regiment partly perhaps to emulate Sassoon and Graves and partly because he himself did recognise his Welsh blood and Wales as a land of soldiers and poets. He later said that England should treasure its Celtic inheritance, 'The blood that makes the poets sing and the prophets see'. The Welsh tradition in poetry was like his own poetry, musical and elegiac. He held the Victorian view that imagination and emotional intelligence were a Celtic endowment. Some of his poetry echoed the musical qualities of ancient Welsh verse. Even during the action in which he won his Military Cross in 1918 he remembered those earlier soldiers, "My forefathers, the agile Welshmen of the mountains".

If we are to probe the beginnings of Owen's artistic ambitions, he certainly was an enthusiastic student of literature at school. He was particularly keen on Wordsworth and studied Shakespeare. There is no evidence that he wrote any serious verse much before 1911 after he left school and then he became devoted to Keats, although this might be exaggerated. Two thirds of his library at school and later could be classified as English Literature; Shakespeare, Scott, Keats and Dickens were the most prominent although it is interesting that he had a number of Bibles. By temperament and education he was exactly suited to become a poet. He had a love of nature, believed in the imagination and had sympathy with those who suffered. In many ways he was a traditional Romantic. He seemed to need solitude and darkness to him was often dazzling. When he became unpaid assistant to the Vicar of Dunstan in Reading, he began to take against the form of Evangelism promoted there. It was not really his mother's Evangelism which was in many ways kindly and natural; it was more stark and dogmatic. He was enthusiastic for the sciences, especially Geology, and, although religion had only a minor part to play in the motivation of his poetry, he tried to reconcile the two. He left the vicarage not long before his twentieth birthday. He saw the Christian religion as only one path among many.

He was in France at the beginning of the war and therefore had not been subject to the same propaganda and so took time to reconcile himself to the need to become a soldier. His disillusion with religion was reinforced by the support which churches gave to the war and the treatment of individuals as cannon fodder. In many ways fitting in with later Romanticism, he held that the exclusive goal of art was beauty and that poetry should be a representation of this. His training as a Romantic had attuned his creative imagination to war and gave him the imagery with which to tackle its uniqueness. He did believe that Germany had to be resisted and that German aggression was ruthless. He had read 'The Song of Roland' and the chivalry that surrounded this great stand in the mountains.

Even from the start of his time in the trenches, he was concerned with poetry but perhaps it was not really until he met Sassoon and gained confidence from the latter's friendship and advice that his poetry really took off. He did use the soldier Christ image in his poetry but many felt that this was more sentimental than Christian. He believed front-line soldiers were heroes and martyrs, most beautiful in death. His mother was an enormous influence on him all through the years. She was always there for him and always supported him. He maintained an ache for home until he finally accepted in the war that he could no longer be 'Harboured in Heaven'.

He knew the pain of the soldiers and he felt the great pity of war. He felt he was a spokesman for the speechless sufferers and he was anxious to plead for the soldiers who had no voice. His shell shock was partly caused by falling into a ruined cellar, "I lost count of days in that cellar and even missed the passing of night and daylight because my only light was a candle". Later, under intense shelling he sheltered in a hole just big enough to lie in, near an officer who had been blown to pieces some weeks earlier. As he says, 'Extra for me there is the universal purvey of ugliness, hideous landscapes, vile noises, foul language, everything unnatural broken, blasted; the distortion of the dead whose unburiable bodies sit outside the dugouts all day, all night, the most execrate sights on earth. In poetry we call them glorious.'

He was sent home suffering from shell shock, surrounded by some rumours of cowardice and was sent to Craiglockhart hospital just outside Edinburgh on 26th June, 1917. He was in hospital for six months and unfit for active service for another nine. He suffered some of the common symptoms of shell shock, the usual sweating of palms and scalp and uncontrollable shaking. Other common symptoms were a rapid pulse, a sense of suffocation, temporary paralysis, acute depression and terrifying dreams. He didn't go mad but he began to get his imagination under some kind of control and increasingly wrote with self-discipline and serenity. The images in his poems were dark with much blood and guilt. His doctor at Craiglockhart, A. J. Brock, helped him enormously. He believed in activity and social interaction and encouraged these very much in Owen. It is thought that Brock encouraged his writing as a therapeutic exercise and 'Dulce and Decorum Est' was begun at the hospital although other poems such as 'Strange Meeting' and 'Mental Cases' were written after he left. Sassoon taught him to think for himself especially in his thoughts about the war and politics. He taught him to use his experience and be true to it in his poetry. As he says, 'I think every poem and every figure of speech should be a matter of experience'. Pity and the understanding of war with regard to the soldiers and its description in his poems were emphasised to undermine the complacency and smugness of civilians in their attitudes towards the war. He believed that the poet's long term aim was to bring healing and peace to the world. By the time he went back to the front in

1918, he was firmly committed to his soldiers and his duty in war. His soul was penetrated by it. In 'Disabled', the mutilated soldier lost all his physical beauty. The poem adds beauty to that which is most deformed until all become aware that this is a fellow human being fit to be loved. The greatest destruction of war was that of youth and beauty. It is common knowledge that he appreciated young male beauty which he saw in many of the soldiers. Again, in 'Greater Love' in 1918, he compares dying soldiers with Christ and affirms that they too are crucified for the redemption of others. There is no evidence that he acknowledged the divinity of Christ but was fascinated by the metaphor. His three great experiences at the front had been fifty hours in a flooded dugout where the sentry was blinded, secondly his fall into the cellar and, thirdly, his sheltering in the hole on the railway embankment. He was determined to prove himself as a soldier and he did so by being awarded the Military Cross for gallantry and he did so in the last months of the war. His aim was to speak for the common man and the soldier. His poetry came out of darkness but spoke of gallantry and saintliness, part of which came out of his own serenity when he eventually came to terms with his own part in the war.

When he went back after Craiglockhart, he was put in charge of 16 Platoon D Company Second Manchesters. After that, he won his citation for a Military Cross by personally manipulating a captured machine gun under fire using it to inflict considerable losses on the enemy. On 3rd October at 5 in the morning, Owen used his knowledge of astronomy and led the company out by the stars. He led the remnants of the company back to safety after they had been right at the point of the attack. Like Sassoon, he had made the welfare of his men his first concern. He said, 'I came out in order to help these boys directly by leading them as well as an officer can, indirectly, by watching their sufferings that I may speak of them as well as a pleader can'. One of his men in a letter home said, 'Do you know that that little officer called Owen who was at Scarborough, he is commanding my company and he is a toff I can tell you - 'No napoo comprec,' which was interpreted as 'A Fine Fellow'. Another letter said that Owen was 'such a decent chap'. His men obviously appreciated him, and he them, in the finest traditions of an officer's profession. He captured brilliantly their sufferings in his poetry.

Two of his greatest poems are:

'Dulce et Decorum Est'

Bent double, like old beggars under sacks,
Knock-kneed, coughing like hags, we cursed through sludge,
Till on the haunting flares we turned our backs
And towards our distant rest began to trudge.
Men marched asleep. Many had lost their boots
But limped on, blood-shod. All went lame; all blind;
Drunk with fatigue; deaf even to the hoots
Of tired, outstripped Five-Nines that dropped behind.

Gas! Gas! Quick, boys! - An ecstasy of fumbling,
Fitting the clumsy helmets just in time;
But someone still was yelling out and stumbling,
And flound'ring like a man in fire or lime...
Dim, through the misty panes and thick green light,
As under a green sea, I saw him drowning.

and:

'Anthem for Doomed Youth'

      What passing-bells for these who die as cattle?
–   *- only the monstrous anger of the guns.*
–   *Only the stuttering rifles' rapid rattle*
–   *can patter out their hasty orisons.*
–   *No mockeries now for them; no prayers nor bells;*
–   *nor any voice of mourning save the choirs, -*
–   *the shrill, demented choirs of wailing shells;*
–   *and bugles calling for them from sad shires.*

What candles may be held to speed them all?
Not in the hands of boys, but in their eyes
shall shine the holy glimmers of good-byes.
The pallor of girls' brows shall be their pall;
their flowers the tenderness of patient minds,
and each slow dusk a drawing-down of blinds.

'The Poems of Wilfred Owen' edited by John Stalworthy
'Owen the Poet' by Domionic Hibberd
'Wilfred Owen, a new Biography 'by D Hibberd
'Wilfred Owen , the Last Year' by D Hibberd
'Wilfred Owen, War Poems and Others' by D Hibberd

OWEN AND SHELL SHOCK

The army report of the War Office on Shell Shock discussed 28,533 official cases occurring in the British Armed Forces form 1914 until the close of 1917. Many people believed the figure was far too low and estimated the number of shell shock victims as 80,000. Owen was hospitalised in April 1917 for shell shock in Scotland where he met Sassoon. His therapy was administered by Dr Arthur Brock, who worked in the same hospital at Craiglockhart as the famous Dr Rivers, who looked after Sassoon. Neither Owen nor Sassoon was reduced to complete psychological ruin or isolation which both of them saw around them in the mental hospital, and both were subject to some sort of recovery.

The War Office broke cases of shell shock down into three classes.
1. General Concussion without visible wound as a result of shell explosion; the cases of these were limited.
2. Emotional shock, either acute in men with a neuropathic predisposition or developing slowly as a result of prolonged strain and terrifying experience, the final breakdown being sometimes brought about by some relatively trivial cause.
3. Nervous and mental exhaustion, the result of prolonged strain and hardship.

As the war dragged on, there was a certain pacifity in the situation of the average soldier. He was often in a prolonged state of waiting to be shot and injured, and because of the range of modern weaponry, although often at a distance from the enemy, he was often in anticipation of bullet or mortar fire. It is not surprising that early cases of shell shock were deemed cowardice, but the psychiatrists soon realised that the symptoms were outside the soldiers' conscious control. Rivers, Sassoon's doctor, said the affliction could be roughly fitted into hysterical disorders and anxiety states.

According to Rivers, it is a striking fact that officers are especially prone to the occurrence of anxiety states, while privates are the chief victims of hysterical manifestations. The ratio of officers to men at the front was approximately 1:30; among the wounded it was 1:24; among the patients admitted to the hospitals for war neuroses in England during the year ended April 30th 1917 it was 1:6. The toll on the officer was especially in evidence because he felt his duty not to let down his men, or show any sign of cowardice. Rivers was especially conscious that many of his patients would never live a normal life again, many ignorant of the realities, regarding shell shock as the soldier's attempt to avoid his duties. On 7th November, 1918, just after Owen died, the last British soldier was shot for desertion. Rivers educated his patients in methods of altering the memory, in order to cope with its horrifying content. He was keen on enabling patients to grieve their losses. He tried to give his patients control over their war experience. He was highly interested in dreams, and encouraged the writing of poetry. Certainly with Owen, his development of his poetry encouraged his recovery. Owen had a bad stammer on his arrival at Craiglockhart, which quickly disappeared as therapy was provided.

Dr Rivers was a man of remarkable education and experience. When he first became involved with the treatment of war traumas, he was confronted with a struggle on two fronts. One was scientific and medical, recognising and learning to relive the stress symptoms; the other was against public and official opinion, which held that any British soldier who quit fighting or otherwise behaved in an unmilitary manner, was a coward and a disgrace.

In talking about Craiglockhart, Rivers writes, 'The bedrooms at the hospital were small and most of them accomodated two or three patients. I was in the habit of giving much thought to the suitability to one another of patients who occupied the same room. I tried to arrange not only that they were men who would get on well together, but also that there was an agreement on such points as their times of getting to sleep, their need for a light at night, and similar points of their cases.

When Robert Graves brought Siegfried Sassoon to Craiglockhart and started talking to Rivers, he immediately took a liking to him. To Sassoon, Rivers was the major figure at the hospital. Sassoon wrote once in his diary, 'I should like to meet Rivers in the next world. It is difficult to believe that such a man as he could be extinguished'. Sassoon wrote, 'Three evenings a week I went along to Rivers' room to give my anti war complex an airing. We talked a lot about war politicians and what they were saying.

I can visualise him sitting at his table in the late summer twilight with his spectacles pushed upon his forehead, and his hands clasped in front of one knee, always communicating his integrity of mind, never revealing that he was weary as he must often have been after long days of exceptionally tiring work on those war neuroses, which demanded such an exercise of sympathy and attachment combined.' At the end of his stay at Craiglockhart, Sassoon said about Rivers, 'Shutting the door of his room for the last time, I left behind me someone who had helped and understood me more than anyone I had ever known. Much as he disliked speeding me back to the trenches, he realised that it was the only way out and the longer I live the more right I know him to have been.'

EDWARD THOMAS

PHILIP Edward Thomas was born in Lambeth on 3 March, 1878, the eldest son of Philip Henry and Mary Elizabeth Thomas. Edward resembled his mother in many ways in that she was retiring and shy and often given to melancholia. She was also dominated by her husband who had an ambitious personality. His father, having left his home town in Tredegar, had made his way in the civil service and was a Welsh speaker, a staunch Liberal and an ardent follower of Lloyd George. Thomas was sent to a number of schools and was pushed repressively by his father. When he left school, he was determined to write and ended up, primarily, as a prose writer. By 1913 he had published twenty prose books under his own name and had edited or introduced a dozen more. About seventy of his articles had been printed in magazines and he had well in excess of 1,500 signed book reviews. He was a striking man, six foot tall, slim and vigorous, with thick long fair hair and a narrow face with strong cheek bones. He had grey blue eyes which were steady but as sharp as a cat's. He rarely laughed and his demeanor was often grave and distant. He often smoked a short clay pipe and was happier with individuals than in groups. His only novel, 'The Happy Go Lucky Morgans 'was dedicated to his parents. It was a semi-autobiographical tale about a Ballam family of Welsh ancestry which included the descriptions of the countryside in South Wales where he had often travelled as a boy. He once said he was five eighths Welsh although he never spoke the language or lived in Wales. At twenty one he wrote of the country as a calling, 'It is like a home sickness but stronger than any homesickness I ever felt, stronger than any passion'. For much of his life until the war, Wales held an almost mystical draw for him, although by 3 September, 1914 he said , 'I am slowly growing into a real Englishman'. There is no doubt that the English countryside had an enormous effect on him and, when it came to defining his patriotism before he went to war, he reflected on his love for England and especially the freedom it brought.

He could be a kind man and in his association with many poets proved a good friend to his countryman W H Davies, paying for his rent and providing him with furniture and every comfort Thomas himself could afford. His first poem was written in November 1914. He had been partially inspired by Robert Frost who became his friend but he felt his poetry was better than his prose and other people found it full of character and insight. According to Walter de La Mare his chief desire was to express himself and his own truth. Walter de La Mare talks about his compassionate and kind heart and his fine, lucid and grave mind and to be alone with him was, 'A grey touchstone of everything artificial and shallow, of everything sweet and natural in the world in which we live'. His poetry was full of the rhythms of speech and of thought and of song and reflected often the conditions of the weather and seasons and the space of the natural world. He wrote many poems over a period of two years after 1914 but the war was often only mentioned obliquely in terms of those missing from the countryside. He would never write of or from the trenches.

There was a down side to Thomas's character. He was diagnosed with the equivalent of depression and often took this out quite cruelly on his family and especially his wife Helen. A lot of his anxiety was based partially on a lack of self-confidence and partially because of various incidents that had taken place in his life, because he felt the need to prove that he was not a coward. This started when his father accused him of cowardice after he had dropped out of a race at St Paul's School. He also felt he had been cowardly as a reviewer when he wrote a glowing account of Ezra Pound's poetry but recanted, withdrawing his approval when he discovered the British literary establishment disliked Pound. Also when he and Frost were neighbours in Gloucestershire and were walking in the woods they were stopped by a gamekeeper with a gun. Frost stood his ground but Thomas retreated and never forgave himself.

This fear of cowardice was a strong motive to join up and, on 23 November, 1915 Thomas was given a commission as Second Lieutenant in the Royal Artillery. They set off for France and the six officers in the battery got on well, often having merry evenings when sometimes Thomas cooked for them all. During the travel through France he had a manservant and life was relatively comfortable until he reached the front line. He came under fire for the first time on 26 February, 1916. He had gone to Agincourt to inspect whether a gun position was visible to the Germans. It must have been, for machine gun bullets whistled overhead accompanied by shell bursts. He wrote to his wife Helen that the experience made him feel shy yet eager to carry on, as far a possible, as though nothing had happened. He said, 'There is no safe place and, consequently, why worry?'. Later he wrote that he no longer wanted anything, 'except I suppose the end'. He said he sometimes wondered why some men get hit and some don't, 'But it is the same with trees and houses so that I don't see why it makes some people believe in God.' He said it's a good thing to believe, 'I think all brave people believe in something'. On 26th, he was supervising the bending and cutting of branches which lay in the battery's line of fire. In the lighthearted atmosphere he noted the kindness that was shown between the men, sharing their lunch packs.

Edward Thomas spent the day before he died under particularly heavy bombardment. He died at Arras on Easter Monday, 1917. A shell passed so close to him that a blast of air stopped his heart and he fell without a mark on his body. In the last page of his war diary he said, ' I never understand quite what is meant by God.' He talked about, 'A road shining like a river uphill after rain, where any turn may lead to Heaven or any corner might hide hell.' He was a man who developed great insights both about other men and things at firsthand rather than facts at second or third. His words came from a heart and mind devoted throughout his life to all that can make the world a decent and natural and lovely place.

Two of Edward Thomas's famous poems are:

'Lights Out'
I have come to the borders of sleep,
The unfathomable deep
Forest where all must lose
Their way, however straight,

Or winding, soon or late;
They cannot choose…

Here love ends,
Despair, ambition ends,
All pleasure and trouble,
Although most sweet or bitter,
Here ends in sleep that is sweeter
Than tasks most noble…

'A Private'

This ploughman dead in battle slept out of doors
Many a frozen night, and merrily
Answered staid drinkers, good bedmen, and all bores:
'At Mrs. Greenland's Hawthorn Bush', said he,
'I slept.' None knew which bush. Above the town,
Beyond 'The Drover', a hundred spot the down
In Wiltshire. And where now at last he sleeps
More sound in France – that, too, he secret keeps.

'Now all Roads lead to France, the last Years of Edward Thomas'
by Matthew Hollis
'Edward Thomas, Collected Poems' with a foreword by Walter de la Mere
'The Poetry of Edward Thomas ' by Andrew Motion

DAVID JONES

1895 – 1974

43

D AVID Jones was a poet and a visual artist. Kenneth Clark thought him the best modern painter. He saw more active service in the First World War than any other British war writer. He spent a total of 117 weeks at the front. His poem 'In Parenthesis' was the great epic poem of the First World War and is based on his first seven months in the trenches which ended in the famous assault on Mametz Wood during the Battle of the Somme. Although he was often amusing and anecdotal about his time in the trenches he did, according to close friends, suffer from shell shock or, as we would now call it, 'post traumatic stress disorder'. He eventually became a Catholic and was a man of great Christian faith, a man of great personal warmth and one who loved all things Welsh. His father was a native North Welshman who worked as a printer's overseer for the Christian Herald Company. He tended towards Evangelism and was a lay preacher. His mother was more inclined to High Church Anglicanism. As happened with many others of his generation, the history he was taught in the Brockley School, a suburb of London, tended towards chauvinism. He was taught that the British were always in the right and usually won. In his adolescence he read widely, including the novels of H G Wells and Kipling, and, above all, he loved Mallory and the Tales of King Arthur. At the age of fourteen he left Brockley Road School for the Camberwell School of Arts and Crafts. From the beginning of his life he seemed to identify with his father's side of the family. He developed a love for Wales and Welsh history and the lineage of the great Welsh families. He was a Romantic. He was quite a success at the Camberwell School of Art and learned a lot about the technical side of drawing and was especially influenced by the accomplished A. S. Hartrick who particularly inspired an enthusiasm for drawing.

The latter became a mentor and a father figure in his art. When the war broke out, he was determined to enlist in a Welsh regiment. He was advised against the Royal Welsh Yeomanry because he didn't know enough about horses. He was inspired by Lloyd George's drive to create a Welsh army corps of two divisions which would contain a London Welsh battalion in which Jones enlisted. Many of the men were Cockneys but all the officers were Welsh. The battalion mustered at Llandudno, which gave Jones an excellent opportunity to study his Welsh connections. One of the things he liked about the army was that it freed him from practical anxieties and tricky choices. The comradeship and warmth this provided appealed to him more than anything else about the army. Although his own regiment was mainly Cockney, the other battalions in the brigade consisted mainly of Welshmen. In the army his romantic feeling for Wales was increased and he noticed his fellow Welshmen seemed to have a greater awareness of history than a lot of their English counterparts. Jones was quite a small man and he found the rigours of marching very difficult but plenty of people helped him out. In February 1916 the battalion headed for the front line near Richebourg. One of the things he noticed more than anything else in the trenches was the awful smell of the bluish grey slime which covered the war-torn earth. Initially, he didn't find life in the trenches too bad and he tended to notice beauty in ordinary things. He talked mostly in the dugouts with small groups from his own platoon. He was often frightened but kept this to himself in order not to let down his mates.

One stormy night he was on sentry duty in a trench at Richebourg-le-Aboue when out of the blue appeared his commander Brigadier General Price-Davies who was an absolute stickler for all regulations including those involving the height of trenches. Price-Davies made them rebuild the trench and all were impressed by the Brigadier General's fearlessness in the face of fire. This fearlessness won him the Victoria Cross and the Distinguished Service Order in South Africa. Jones's feelings for junior officers were not entirely friendly and even more so for men of Price-Davies's rank. The Welsh were often critical of their officers especially if they found them unfeeling and incompetent. Jones was once asked by the battalion commander, Colonel Bell, why he didn't apply to become an officer, but Jones was having none of it. He didn't like responsibility and although certainly not a coward, having shown himself a competent soldier after six months of combat, he didn't want to put himself in front of the men. He was a huge admirer of courage which is probably the virtue he praised more than any other. His nemesis came on about the ninth of July, 1915, when the battalion was to take part in the general attack on Mametz Wood with the entire division. There had already been an attack on the wood which had failed and lead to the replacement of the divisional commander, Major General Ivor Philips. The attack was massive and, in the advance, he heard one of the most moving things he ever heard - the 14th Battalion, singing in Welsh, 'Jesu Lover of my Soul'. He was shot in the calf, half an inch behind the bone; he was eventually picked up and rescued and sent back to Blighty. Jones, looking back on his experience now as an old soldier, felt very unsettled while recuperating at home. But he returned to France in late October 1915. He became aware that the war had changed. He had lost many friends who had been replaced by strangers and he was transferred from the front line to battalion headquarters where his job was to help make sketch maps and later to plot coordinates to pinpoint German batteries. He was forever cold when soldiering and spent much of his time looking for wood and, one day, he spotted a byre and going up to it, he looked through the gap in the wall and saw two gusty candle flames and there before them he saw a chaplain in an alb and a short gold coloured chasuble facing a stack of ammunition boxes covered by a white cloth. There were half a dozen infantrymen kneeling before it. One of these soldiers was a hard-drinking, hard-fighting Irishman and Jones had never seen anything like this in the Anglican Church. It was a Catholic service and reflected the huge power and ritual of communion in Roman Catholicism.

It was an experience he never forgot and it stayed in his mind forever. A slightly more amusing experience was when he was in a communication trench and suddenly found himself face to face with the Prince of Wales. He pointed the Prince in the right direction and, after the Prince had gone, around the corner came a very red-faced and out-of-sorts colonel who asked him, 'Have you seen Wales?' Jones was very amused. Before the Battle of Passchendale he was assigned to an Italian reserve force which was out of the front line. Jones was quite upset at this as he had to leave his friends but he had no choice. To Jones the destruction and boredom of war seemed to reflect an emptiness in life. The actual involvement in war, the heroism, the patience and love between soldiers was ultimately spiritual but his Anglican

Christianity never really provided him with the spiritual fulfilment he needed. He became a Roman Catholic. He was drawing all the time and one of the drawings and writings he became well known for was entitled, 'The Quest'. This reflected his annoyance with the inequality of military rank and the class system and reveals a liking for William Morris type socialism. He disliked the war but was prepared to soldier on but he was suffering to some degree from shell shock. He was, probably, neurasthenic when anxiety gradually increased, often resulting in a breakdown sometimes delayed until many years later. Many of these ex-servicemen were prevented by their lingering neurosis from leading productive lives. Many ended up unemployed and some committed suicide. Eventually he got trench fever and was taken out of combat. When, eventually, he went back to the battalion they were in Ireland. Here he had some intuition into the great fissures that run through that country. He experienced a Celtic temperament different from that of the Welsh. The Irish were light-hearted and optimistic and seemed to find that everything had a funny side to it.

In 1932, after the war and after his demobilisation, Jones finished, 'In Parenthesis'. The great illusions in the poem align the Battle of the Somme with the defeat of Roland at Roncesvalles and also the Battle of Camlan which brought to an end Arthur's Celtic Britain. The poem was slow to be recognised although T. S. Eliot considered it a deeply moving work of genius and W. H. Auden declared it a masterpiece and in 1954 the greatest book about the First World War. In 1980 Graham Greene judged it among the greatest poems of the century. However, after his friend Douglas Clevendon's radio broadcast of the poem in 1947, he suffered a second crushing breakdown. He was given treatment by a skilled therapist called Bill Stevenson who told him that he had been more frightened during the war than he had realised and urged him to return to visual art and continue writing. On 15th July 1964 he met and had a long talk with Siegfried Sassoon and they shared experiences. In 1974 he was made a Companion of Honour and on the 28th October 1974 he died in his bed. He was a man of huge depth, complicated but with a great sense of history and an appreciation of the Celtic temperament. He was not a man who grudged his time in the army but emphasised the good qualities and virtues that he had seen. Like many distinguished artists he abhorred war but was prepared to fight for his country. Now that he is dead many of us throughout the Welsh artistic scene realise he was one of our jewels in the crown in the twentieth century. He was a great Welshman and we salute him.

'Reading David Jones' by Thomas Dilworth
'The Long Conversation', a memoir of David Jones by William Blisset
'David Jones in the Great War' by Thomas Dilworth

HEDD WYN

ON November 16th 1886 Evan Evans, the son of a farmer, married Mary Morris, a maidservant at Maentwrog, Merionethshire. He was older than his bride by about ten years. On January 13th 1887 Mary gave birth to their first born child, a son whom they named Ellis Humphrey Evans who eventually became known throughout the whole of Wales by his bardic name, Hedd Wyn. The family was quite large, consisting of eight children, although some of them died at an early age. They farmed Yr Ysgwrn which was a hard life but was self sufficient. Hedd Wyn's education was fairly spasmodic and he left school at fourteen. At twenty-one he did go down to Abercynon to seek his fortune in the colliery but soon saw through the illusion of gold in the coalfield and returned home. At the age of eleven he had been inspired by J.D. Richards, the minister of the local chapel, to read poetry, especially that in Welsh under the rules of strict meter which he soon mastered. He won his first prize at a literary meeting held at Trawsfynydd when he was twelve years old. In 1907 he won his first chair at the Bala Eisteddfod. His reputation grew as a local poet and competitor at eisteddfodau. It was at this time that a local compere gave him his bardic name, Hedd Wyn, Hedd meaning peace and Gwyn meaning white or holy. Another literary friend who helped him greatly was William Morris, a native of Blaenau Ffestiniog, who enrolled in Bala Theological College. Hedd Wyn was quite shy and felt rather inadequate with educated people but that did not stop him being influenced by them and spending time in their company. In 1913 he was becoming well known in the literary circles of his day and he won several prizes in local eisteddfodau. He was never a great farmer or shepherd because so often he would drift into contemplation rather than action. As he grew older he began to court women and had a number of interesting relationships. As a youth, he helped his father on the farm, was immersed in his own world which was peaceful and friendly but was soon to be destroyed by the First World War.

His attitude, initially, towards the war was one of apathy; however, some of his friends were killed, and he turned away from jingoistic poems to ones describing the horror of war as a new starkness and realism crept into them. His most famous war poem is, 'War' and those and other poems gave ample evidence to show that he was against warfare.

Here is part of that poem in both Welsh and English.

'Rhyfel'

Gwae fi fy myw mewn oes mor ddreng,
A Duw ar drai ar orwel pell;
O'i ôl mae dyn, yn deyrn a gwreng,
Yn codi ei awdurdod hell.

Pan deimlodd fyned ymaith Dduw
Cyfododd gledd i ladd ei frawd;
Mae s?n yr ynladd ar ein clyw,
A'i gysgod ar fythynnod tlawd.
Mae'r hen delynau genid gynt
Ynghrog ar gangau'r helyg draw,
A gwaedd y bechgyn lond y gwynt,
A'u gwaed yn gymysg efo'r glaw.

'War'

Why must I live in this grim age,
When, to a far horizon, God
Has ebbed away, and man, with rage,
Now wields the sceptre and the rod?

Man raised the sword, once God had gone,
To slay his brother, and the roar
Of battlefields now casts upon
Our homes the shadow of the war.

The harps to which we sang are hung
On willow boughs, and their refrain
Drowned by the anguish of the young
Whose blood is mingled with the rain.

When new legislation came into force at the beginning of 1916 forcing single men of a certain age into service, the family were faced with an incredibly cruel choice. Either he or his brother could remain at home. He decided to join up, a brave choice. He joined the 15th Battalion of the Royal Welch Fusiliers, and was declared fit to serve in the forces. He travelled to Liverpool station and to Litherland camp, a drab and cheerless place. It is interesting that both Sassoon and Graves were both at Litherland but never met Hedd Wyn. According to one of his friends he was an inept soldier, always rather idle and untidy. He was often shouted at by sergeants but, at the same time, because he was a poet some allowance was made. Here he started writing the poem 'The Hero' for the 1917 National Eisteddfod.

He put an enormous amount of work into it and we shall see later how it got on. On June 9th he departed for France. He had not received more than three months training. He saw his home for the last time on leave at the beginning of June. By the second week of June he was at Rouen in France. From here, in one of his letters he wrote that, 'Beauty is stronger than war and that loveliness will outlive the sadness. But the flowers of France in the future will be flowers of sadness and a sad wind will blow over the land because the flowers will be of the colour of blood and the wind will be full of the sound of mourning'. Hedd Wyn spent the last days of his life at a camp on the banks of the Yser near Ypres. The battalion was dispatched to take part in a great offensive, crossing the Yser canal on July 29th. Their objective was to capture the village of Pilkham. The campaign was an awful mess, the weather terrible and the ground waterlogged. The battle became known as Passchendale. The battle fought on July 31st was nothing more than a massacre. Hedd Wyn, in a mad rush through the horrors of No Man's Land, was seen to fall after a shell had burst in the midst and although he lay there wounded, not groaning or uttering a sigh, he died on a stretcher.

His commanding officer said he fought extremely well and he was always in the thick of the fighting. His loss was a tragedy. He was a poetic genius, kind and humble, friendly with everybody. His death was followed by the remarkable victory of his poem 'The Hero' in the Birkenhead National

Eisteddfod. Even today on the first Monday of every month in a cafe in Belgium the Welsh flag is solemnly raised. It marks the spot where the Welsh poet Hedd Wyn was killed. These days it is the location of a cafe called De Sportsman. The interior is covered with the Welsh flag and other memorabilia. Each month the owner plays two or three songs on the trumpet and gives out freshly baked cakes to customers to remember Hedd Wyn and all the Welsh people who died around the cafe. The owner says, 'We have a plaque dedicated to him with flowers and his picture'. Hedd Wyn has become more than a war poet in Belgium. He has become a link between the Flemish and the Welsh, two small nations who wish to preserve their culture in a united Europe moving towards a shining peace.

'The Story of Hedd Wyn, the poet of the Black Chair' by Alan Llwyd

SIEGFRIED SASSOON

SIEGFRIED Lorraine Sassoon was born in 1886 in the lovely and unspoilt Weald of Kent. His mother adored him and was an extraordinary woman, a good artist and committed Anglican. Unfortunately, she and his father separated before his fifth birthday and certainly Siegfried became very depressed when his father died in April 1905. He was sent to Marlborough College where he learnt one of the great loves of his life which was cricket. Coming from a country house background, he also indulged in fox hunting and later went on to compete in point to points where his bravery was unquestioned. He went on playing cricket until his 70s playing for the Ravens at Downside. He also enjoyed golf but hunting was not so much of an obsession after the war. His home and school helped produce a love of literature and old books and that, with a great enjoyment of the countryside, produced in him the fervent wish to become a poet. When he left school in autumn 1905, he went up to Cambridge. His two brothers were at Clare College which he joined.

He decided to read law but he hated the dryness of academics and, as a consequence, he lost interest in his degree and gave up Cambridge. He settled into a life of poet, sportsman and country gentleman with a private income. He made contacts with literary London and some of his verse was published. He had a great love of music and began to explore in a fairly cerebral way his tendency to homosexuality. He mixed through introductions with many of the literati of his time. When war was declared on 4 August 1914 he became a trooper in C Squadron 1st Battalion the Sussex Yeomanry, the Royal Sussex Regiment. He certainly had none of the attributes of his fellow soldiers but found his compatriots kind and helpful. One of his friends, Bobby Hanmer, from an old Welsh family was joining the Royal Welch Fusiliers. Sassoon wrote to the adjutant of that regiment who sent a positive reply suggesting he join the regiment in May. In many ways, as a young officer, he was naïve and idealistic. His background had made him something of an innocent. He always had a sense of the supernatural and, maybe, he had the genes from the Jewish prophets. To him the war became the world's worst wound. He reflected its awfulness and its tragedy. This was his declaration, which was to be read out in the House of Commons and which caused him, through Graves's intervention, to be sent to Craiglockhart.

A Soldier's declaration

I am making this statement as an act of wilful defiance of military authority, because I believe the war is being deliberately prolonged by those who have the power to end it.

I am a soldier, convinced that I am acting on behalf of soldiers. I believe that this war, upon which I entered as a war of defence and liberation, has now become a war of aggression and conquest. I believe that the purposes for which I and my fellow soldiers entered upon this war should have been so clearly stated as to have made it impossible to change them, and that, had this been done, the objects which actuated us would now be attainable by negotiation.

I have seen and endured the suffering of the troops, and I can no longer be a party to prolong these sufferings for ends which I believe to be evil and unjust.

I am not protesting against the conduct of the war, but against the political errors and insincerities for which the fighting men are being sacrificed.

On behalf of those who are suffering now I make this protest against the deception which is being practised on them; also I believe that I may help to destroy the callous complacence with which the majority of those at home regard the continuance of agonies which they do not share, and which they have not sufficient imagination to realise.

S Sassoon
July 1917

I cannot relay much of Sassoon's poetry here because he hasn't been dead 70 years but I just repeat his poem,

'The General'

"Good morning, good morning," the general said,
When we met him last week on his way to the line

Now the soldiers he smiled at are most of 'em dead
And we're cursing his staff for incompetent swine.
"He's a cheery old card'" grunted Harry to Jack
As they slogged up to Arras with rifle and pack
But he did for them both with his plan of attack.

Like other young men of his time, especially those from public schools, he
developed for the most part Platonic love for some of his contemporaries.
He was devastated when his lovely friend, David Thomas, from my old school
Christ College, Brecon, was killed. The resulting fury that it caused him
made him quite reckless in the front line leading to the award of a Military
Cross. Going back on leave and mixing in literary and some pacifist circles,
he came to question the 'raison d'etre' of the war. His letter of protest to the
government sparked off a reaction when he was partly saved by his friend,
Robert Graves, who suggested to the board of enquiry that he should go to
the mental hospital at Craiglockhart in Edinburgh and so he avoided a court
martial. There he was attended to by Captain W. Rivers whom we have
already talked about in the essay discussing Wilfred Owen. The work of
Rivers and Dr Brock was quite pioneering. Rivers allowed him to talk about
himself and the statement on the war that he had made and Rivers listened
and was never judgemental. Rivers recognised in Sassoon an imbalance
tending towards self-sacrifice rather than self-preservation. At the hydro
Rivers encouraged both Owen and Sassoon to take part in normal activities
and to socialise outside the hospital. Owen's poetry was very different from
Sassoon's but they could both rise to poems of lyric beauty. They both pitied
their fellow soldiers and, above all, Sassoon wanted to stand by his soldiers;
this was echoed in a piece of prose,

"I was standing beside Corporal Griffith who had his elbows on the dew
soaked parapet. His face visible in the sinking light of a flare had the look of
a man who was doing his simple duty without demanding explanations from
the star above him, vigilant and serious he stared straight ahead of him and
a fine picture of fortitude he made. He was only a stolid young farmer from
Montgomeryshire; but such men I think were England in those dreadful years
of war."

Today we would probably say 'England and Wales, or Britain'. There is little to suggest that, at this stage, Sassoon was a highly religious man, but he went on to convert to Catholicism and became much more religious in his later life. But he was a spiritual man and was attracted to such people as T.E. Lawrence, the subject of another essay here, and, in the weeks before the Armistice, after they had met and formed a friendship, Sassoon recalled: 'The impression left on me by Lawrence was of a pleasant, unassuming person who preferred to let other people do most of the talking. As he often did, he was subduing that power of stimulation which could lift others above and beyond their habitual plane of thought and action by communicating his mysterious and superlative vital energy. Had I been told that I was meeting one of the most extraordinary beings I should ever know and idolise, I should have refused to believe it.' He did marry, but it was not a happy marriage. Dennis Silk, a friend of the author's uncle and of Sassoon writes: 'Whenever I think of Siegfried now I see an over-coated, pipe-smoking figure seated in a deckchair under the Haytesbury's lovely south front. I think of one whose spiritual pilgrimage had taken him, in Maurice Wiggin's words,

'Out of the Old Century',

Out of the old century, across the weald of youth, over the hard going of middle age to the beckoning coverts wherein he found his peace; galloping and being thrown and always remounting, a rare good plucked 'un, robust and sensitive, brave and kind.' Silk goes on to say, 'I think above all of a man who had learned to be at peace with himself, a man who could live most fully when left alone.

'Memoirs of a Fox Hunting Man' by Siegfried Sassoon
'Memoirs of an Infantry Officer' by S Sassoon
'Selected Poems' by S Sassoon
'Siegfried Sassoon' by John Stuart Roberts
'Siegfried Sassoon and the Great War, the Making of a War Poet'
by Dennis Silk

ROBERT GRAVES

THE name Graves derives from graef, the Norman word for quarry. The family arrived in England between the 12th and 15th Centuries. Graves was born in 1895. His mother was religious and his father was hard-working and public-spirited. His father was Irish and he had a German mother whose surname was Von Ranke. Robert was educated at prep schools and then went to Charterhouse in 1909. His strongest memories of childhood were of Germany and North Wales, where he spent the school holidays. His attachment to Wales was deep. In 1897 his parents Alfred and Amy went on a Welsh holiday and stayed at Harlech.

They bought some land and built a house called 'Erinfa'. This was the start of Robert's romantic attachment to Wales and Celtic literature. His father became immersed in the world of Welsh poetry. Robert's schooling at Charterhouse was not a happy one but he did develop a love for poetry. In the years 1913-14 he started to turn away from his family and was fascinated by the idea of becoming a poet. At Charterhouse Graves had opposed war but, on returning to Harlech, he realised that joining the army would help him to escape from a rather suffocating family atmosphere. The nearest regimental depot belonged to the Royal Welch Fusiliers at Wrexham and the secretary of Harlech golf club helped his entry by explaining that he had been in the school officers' training corps at Charterhouse. The Royal Welch Fusiliers first went into battle in 1690 at the Battle of the Boyne.

They had twenty nine battle honours, one of the longest in the British Army. They wore five black flashes on the backs of their collars, a remnant from the days when pigtails were worn to keep the grease off the uniform. They prided themselves on their smartness which did not help Graves because he was so scruffy. The King had persuaded Kitchener that they could keep their flashes since they were so brave the enemy would never see their backs. They always went into battle accompanied by their long haired white goat which was led around the long mess table at the officers' St David's Day dinner. The most recent young officer would stand on a chair and put one foot on the table before consuming a raw leek and drinking a toast to the roll of drums. On parades the goat would lead the rows of regimental pioneers who marched in white aprons and gauntlets. The 9th Battalion went into the trenches with replica swords of those used at the Battle of Crecy.

The spelling of 'Welch' in Royal Welch Fusiliers and the Royal Welch Regiment is quite enigmatic and requires explanation. In 1702, when the Welsh designation was granted to 23rd Foot, the spelling 'Welch' was in common usage, but this was swept away during the latter half of the nineteenth century by 'Welsh'. In February 1831 a letter was received from Horse Guards directing the 41st Foot style themselves as 'The 41st', or the Welch Regiment of Infantry'. It would appear that on official publications the spelling varied between 'c' and 's' although both regiments stuck resolutely to the old spelling. Matters came to a head in the Great War, when cap badges were produced for the Royal Welch Fusiliers and the Welch Regiment showing 'Welsh'. Once the war was over, it was generally agreed within the two regiments that the traditional spelling was more correct. Consequently, the two Colonels, Lieutenant-General Sir Francis Lloyd and Major-General Sir Thomas Lloyd made application to the Army Board for the re-instatement of the spelling 'Welch'. Official approval for 'Welch' was received from the War Office on 27th January 1920. This explanation does not, however, answer the question as to why 'Welsh' is used in the title of the new regiment 'The Royal Welsh'. The assumption is that the Royal Welch Fusiliers were always colloquially referred to as 'The Royal Welch' and some difference was necessary to set the new regiment apart from one of its constituents. Also, 'Welsh' is in common usage, therefore any mis-spellings would be minimised.

Another custom Graves was interested in was 'The Loyal Toast.' The Loyal Toast was never proposed in the Officers Mess of the Royal Welch Fusiliers except on St David's Day. Furthermore, the officers and their guests did not stand when the band played the national anthem at the conclusion of its programmes. This custom has no written origin but possibly dates from the late eighteenth century. At the time of Mutiny at the Nore in 1797 the mutineers called the Warrant Officers, NCOs and men of the Royal Welch Fusiliers to join them. Their response was to submit an address to the Commanding Officer for forwarding to the King, expressing their unswerving loyalty to the Crown. A copy of their address is in the regimental museum in Caernarvon, and the endorsement by the Commanding Officer verifies that it was signed 'by the whole Corps unanimously'. King George IV, at first as Prince of Wales and then as Prince Regent and also Monarch, would from time to time dine with the regiment. On one of these occasions, no doubt mindful of the regiment's declaration of loyalty during the mutiny, he is said to have expressed the wish that the Loyal Toast should be dispensed with as 'The Loyalty of the Royal Welch is never in doubt'.

It is interesting that the Royal Welch Fusiliers was as full of snobbery as many other infantry regiments, but latterly they came to realise that there were not many public schools in Wales and to get talented officers they would have to spread their net to the comprehensive sector. In terms of snobbery, Sassoon once told Graves that in his battalion of the RWF, the war was considered 'a social inconvenience'. It is also pertinent that certainly one of their commanding officers used to address the assembled battle group as 'Gentlemen of the Royal Welch Fusiliers and men of other regiments'. Graves was taken aback by the lewdness of the men and his intellectual arrogance was not appreciated by some of his fellows. He won compliments from the adjutant 'Tibs' Crawshay but, among his other foibles, his failure to watch Crawshay's horse run in the Grand National counted against him. Graves first arrived in France in May 1915. In September Graves took part in the Loos offensive and was transferred as a special reserve captain to Locon where he first met Sassoon. On the Somme in 1916 he was back in the trenches. He talks about feeling really frightened and said that, 'If happiness consisted of being miserable in a good cause, why then I am doubly happy.' As time went on, he found Sassoon's poetry more congenial and his own first book of poems 'Over the Brazier' was published. He had sustained a boxing injury while training which necessitated time off at Harlech. He was sent back to France in time for the Somme offensive and on 20th was so badly wounded in the attack on High Wood that he was thought to be dead. The wounds turned out not to be life-threatening except for some damage to the right lung. Sassoon was also sent back with lung trouble and they convalesced together at Harlech. Graves was starting to get worried about Sassoon's attitude to the war; however, when Sassoon made his protest, Graves told him he had been very courageous. Graves pressed his old friend Evan Morgan, private secretary to the Minister of Labour, to persuade the War Office to send Sassoon to a Medical Board. Sassoon tended to think Graves was more interested in pursuing good form than in really defying the awfulness of the war and protecting young soldiery. Graves's marriage to Nancy Nicholson took place on 23rd January 1918 at St James's, Piccadilly. Sassoon did not attend and with the writing of 'Goodbye to all That', Graves's story of his time in the First World War, there came an estrangement between the two poets. After the war, Graves was financially insecure and still suffered from shell shock. He frequently called upon Sassoon to provide funds and felt his friend was too stingy. When Graves published his war memoir he included a poem not for publication by Sassoon. Sassoon wrote to Graves telling him that the book had caused him extreme difficulty and discomfort and that it had landed on him like a Zeppelin bomb. With a complete lack of remorse, Graves replied: 'Signing fat cheques for your friends; the indelicate irony of it is that, had you thought of signing one when you heard of my troubles which left us all without money, I would not have been forced to write 'Goodbye to all That' to contribute to the work of restoration and you would not have had the Zeppelin bomb.' The estrangement was complete.

Graves found it easier to get on with the men than the officers in the Royal Welch. However, he rarely identified himself with the officers who were hunting men who rated courage and immaculate dress as being the height of good behaviour. When he first arrived on the Front, he was sent out on patrol which involved a two hour stomach crawl into German territory under barbed wire and enemy flares. He was often reckless in his courage. In that early relationship with Sassoon they often met to talk about poetry and books; Graves in particular was fascinated by ideas. His first poetry was greeted by 'The Times Literary Supplement' as being full of repelling rawness and achieved something like true beauty. However, Sassoon was often creatively critical of his poetry, although, for some time, they were great friends. In late November 1916 Graves and Sassoon shared a hut and edited each other's work. Graves would often sing ballads and do imitations of bubbling and excitable Welshmen. They did discuss religion and Graves preferred the idea of Christ as a God-like man rather than God himself. Graves in fact often described God as a woman. He exhibited all the symptoms of post-traumatic stress both towards the end of the war when he was convalescing and after the war. He was fascinated by William Rivers whom he had been involved with as the psychiatrist who treated Sassoon at Craiglockhart Hospital in 1917. Although he had been encouraged by T.E. Lawrence earlier in the war it was to Rivers he turned and visited the latter's rooms regularly in St John's Cambridge in 1921. Rivers had spent three years working with the war damaged soldiers at Craiglockhart. Rivers told Graves that he should see shell-shock as a gift on which to draw his poetic powers. Rivers was a man of great intellectual depth and breadth and was regarded by many of his contemporaries as having a great mind. In Graves's writing, especially 'Goodbye to all That', he described the love he had felt for his soldiers and that the terrible fear of death was all around him. We probably would describe Graves as a religious man but not one of a conventional bent. He was fascinated by mythology and the supernatural and delved into his own depths of pain and fear to create some marvellous writing. He never ended up in a war hospital for nervous breakdown but came close to it. His physical ailments gave him some time out of the war and probably saved him from this. However, the war was to have a lasting effect on him even though it made him want to live life to the full, having realised his ultimate vulnerability. In many ways he was typical of a breed of officer attracted to the Royal Welch Fusiliers because of its Celtic origins, characteristics and qualities, especially displayed by its soldiers.

Certainly the present day culture of the Royal Welch Fusiliers was one where the officers got on with the men but, in the early years of the last century, there were still huge class differences between them which meant the present day culture was not so prevalent. On 7th December 1985 he died after a long life, much of the latter part spent abroad where he sought to enjoy life to the full.

'Robert Graves, Life on the Edge' by Miranda Seymour
'Robert Graves and the White Goddess' by Richard Percival Graves

CYNAN
1895-1970

CYNAN was very much a patriot. He had been brought up the son of a religious and well-meaning shopkeeper in the small country town of Pwllheli; named Albert Evans Jones, he later included in his own name his bardic pseudonym 'Cynan'. Having graduated at the Bangor Community College in 1916, he went off to join the Welsh student company of the RAMC as a private. He then became a chaplain with the Worcesters. He had the courage to change denominational commitment from being a Baptist to a Methodist. 'Mab y Bwthyn' is one of his early war poems written in Welsh, translated: 'As we wearily tramped along, the mud and rain having killed our song, One thing there was that stirred my mind, by dawn the Somme will be far behind.'

'Wrth Imi drampio'n flin drwy'r llaid,
A'r glaw yn disgyn yn ddi-baid,
Dywedwn wrth fy nghalon drom,
'Byddwn cyn dydd ymhell o'r Somme.'

The Welsh poet set much of his war poetry in a context of Christian sympathy, often drawing a parallel between the soldier's sacrifice and the courage of the three warriors of King David when they broke through the lines of the Gaza regiment to get hold of the water that the leader wanted from the well of Bethlehem. His poem, 'l'Envoi' (I Gymrodyr y Rhyfel Mawr) is a war poem that took the direct form of a ballad and his ballads later became one of his major contributions to Welsh literature. The war ballad, 'Miraglau'r Mor' (Miracles of the Sea) reminds us of the Rhyme of the Ancient Mariner. During his lonely night watch, the sailor talks aloud as he remembers his fallen comrades. He is visited by the war spirit, surrounded by the ghosts of dead soldiers; the former proclaims that he reigns supreme as he invites the dead to the eternal peace of the Isle of Avalon. The sailor questions the dead and, as he prays, the Saviour of mankind approaches over the waters and the ghostly countless legions turn to follow him. The poem was an expression of Cynan's conviction of the saving power of Christianity which could never be destroyed by evil. Later, as the poet surveyed the graves of Welsh soldiers in Flanders, he was reminded of some of the earliest Welsh poetry to be found in the Black

Book of Carmarthen, 'Y Beddau, a'u gwlych I glaw' (The Graves which the Rains Washed). The poet was reminded of the terrible betrayal of the ideals of young soldiers, especially when they came back to that which was not a better land in which to live. The poet hated the hypocritical profit-making which surrounded the war and on this subject he formed his own Cenotaph address, 'Balad Wrth Gofeb i y Milwyr' (A Ballad by the Soldiers' Memorial). It was not a literary exercise; it was wrapped up in sadness and disgust for the exploitation of the soldiers. Cynan was never subject to the disciplining that Sassoon experienced, perhaps because Welsh literature was not perceived of as important, but there is no more terrible indictment of war than Cynan's, 'Byddugoliaeth' (Victory).

In Cynan's poem the dying soldier talks to the padre:
'Known they the cost of victory, Did they see the famished town, Did they see the smoke of burning homes, Where the altar of God looks down; Did they see the lines of hatred that froze black on their lips, Did they see the graves that were nameless, the bodies that coffinless lay?'

'At welsant hwy bris yr ennill?...
...A welsant newyn y dref?
A welsant fwg cartrefi llosg yn esgyn at orsedd nef?...
A Welsant grychau casineb yn rhewi'n ddu ar ei fin.'

Like Sassoon, Cynan believed that the faithful description of war's horrors constituted its most terrible indictment. When he wrote from the dugouts of Salonika and France, Cynan's poems revealed a Christian attitude to life and, despite the carnage, he still believed in Jesus Christ. Despite his despair he retained belief and hope in human life as guided by the great Christian God although, often, he describes the disillusionment in the soldier that destroyed all hope.

('Beth yw ing cariadon heno pan yw'r byd I gyd ar dan?
Wrth arteithiau'r blin genhedloedd, beth yw'n holl helyntion man?')

('With the world itself on fire, what are lover's thoughts tonight?
With the tired nations tortured, what of our pathetic plight?')

Cynan was, undoubtedly, a brave man who endured the trenches and
brought relief to many seriously injured soldiers. He went on to become one
of the great figures in Welsh literature and, although he had been scarred by
war in many ways, it reinforced his integrity and dedication to poetry.

Chaplains were a unique breed in the British Army, the author's father being
one. In wartime they had huge spiritual duties to maintain the high moral
ground of their charges and to encourage them out of the depths of despair.
Cynan was one of the great chaplains of his time.

T. E. LAWRENCE

T.E. Lawrence was born in 1888 in Tremadog, North Wales. His father was Anglo-Irish. Ivor Wynne Jones, author and journalist, has done some research on his mother. Ivor said, when he was chatting in a mixture of Irish and Arabic to an Howeitat chieftain in the Negev somewhere North of Aqaba, 'I told him I was not 'chaskari Ingilizi' but came from Wales', not expecting much response from a desert Bedouin. To my surprise, he said, 'Ah, the same country as Major Lawrence'. More surprising than the Arab's response was the fact that T. E .L. had ever bothered to make the point after leading the poor Hashemites out of the Hejaz into a stateless wilderness. In his research Ivor Wynne Jones says that he came to disregard the information on T. E. L.'s mother's birth certificate and found that his grandfather on his mother's side was John Lawrence born in Monmouth, the son of a Swansea-born mother and a Monmouth-born father. That also gives the origin of the surname 'Lawrence' which, otherwise, would appear to have been plucked out of the air by a father called 'Chapman' and a mother named 'Junar'. You also get the origin of Sarah Junar's Christian name, Sarah Lawrence, who was the mother of Sarah Junar's young father.

In his early boyhood at about the age of five, the family moved from Trebanog to Oxford where he attended Oxford High School. He chose Jesus College as his second choice when trying for Oxford, mainly because he was awarded a Meyricke exhibition to this Welsh College which was a Welsh exhibition which he qualified for by his Welsh birthplace.
From early childhood Lawrence was devoted to books and the subject matter was often castles, especially the medieval history surrounding them and their architecture. He also soon began to take a considerable interest in warfare, both ancient and modern. He was gifted with a terrific memory for detail, especially for countries and their people. Behind all this interest there was a deep introspection and self-consciousness according to his friend Vyvyan Richards. One of his great qualities was a tremendous attachment to personal freedom and the equality of the individual. He was never at college or at school a team man but he certainly was not a bookworm. He was an adventurer and, even at Oxford, explored parts other people did not know existed. Even at this stage in his career he also slept and ate less than most

other people. Not only was he a man of learning but he had remarkable skill with his hands. He always mended things and fine printing was one of the activities that most appealed to him. His attachment to the Ashmolean Museum inspired him to explore the Middle East. Regarding his attachment to Wales and his Welshness, I note that he was said once to have claimed that he came from one of the few countries that had beaten England.

Lawrence, having had much experience in the Middle East, was commissioned near the outbreak of war on October 23 1914. He was a temporary 2nd Lieutenant interpreter and became involved in intelligence. We now come to his relationship with the Arabs. The state of oppression they had suffered under the Turks made a deep impression on him. He wanted to become their champion and rescue a whole people from slavery. In all his affairs, personal affection was one of his highest attributes. He had a number of close and young Arab friends but there was never any evidence that relationships were permeated by physical homosexuality. He soon realised the economic life of the desert was based on the supply of camels which were best nurtured in the hill pastures. This moulded the life of the Bedouin who travelled between the Spring, Summer and Winter pasturages. He realised the Bedouin were a people of black and white whose thoughts tended to dwell on extremes. The sense of freedom that the roaming Bedouin gave to Lawrence and the harshness of their existence, which appealed to his aesthetic side, made him their great companion. He saw them as unstable as water but, like water, they would eventually take over. For a whole year and more from the capture of Aqaba in July 1917 to the capture of Damascus in October 1918 Lawrence had the huge and exacting job of knitting together the wild Bedouin and the trained forces of the British. Lawrence learned very quickly how to accommodate the Arabs. He described their gatherings of chieftains as something between wolves and wayward children and he subtly directed their ideas and learnt their individual foibles. For Lawrence the training and movement across the desert were the most thrilling part of the campaign. The gore and nastiness of the slaughter the Arabs imposed on the Turks he was not keen on. There was an incident with a Turkish official which could have been described as homosexual rape after he was captured but, to this day, we do not know the

truth of the details. As for the inspiration which drove him to write
'The Seven Pillars of Wisdom' there was certainly not much Christian
spirituality behind it as he had always certainly dismissed conventional
Christianity, having had it forced down his throat by his mother. There is
no doubt that he was a man of deep spiritual feeling.

Much of it came from nature especially the desert. He does not seem to
have embraced Islam. He left Arabia, initially dejected at what he saw
was the betrayal of the Arabs by the great powers but, when eventually a
separate Arab kingdom was created, he felt he had been justified and a lot
of the struggle had been worth it. He did not want to be lauded in his native
kingdom of Britain but preferred instead to become a lowly aircraftman in
the RAF. He was delighted and excited by new technologies and machines
and this position allowed him access to them. Having been a war hero, a
distinguished soldier and in rank a full colonel, he was an embarrassment
to the authorities but he believed in personal choice and pursuing his own
destiny. This he was allowed to do up to a point. He wrote his great tome
'Seven Pillars of Wisdom' which made a huge contribution to the history
of the campaign. But he was its greatest critic, feeling that it had never
achieved greatness as a work of art. He once said that a man never amounts
to anything unless he be an artist. No great captain had really portrayed the
inner workings of his spirit in the way Lawrence depicted them in this book.
From the spiritual point of view, he once said, according to his brother the
words: 'I hate Christianity' That never stopped him, however, growing
into a great spirit, a great leader of men and a huge inspiration to the Arab
people whom he loved and whose freedom he pursued relentlessly.

'Hero, the Life and Legend of Lawrence of Arabia' by Michael Korda
'The Seven Pillars of Wisdom', by T E Lawrence
'Lawrence of Arabia, the Selected Letters' edited by Malcolm Brown

SAUNDERS LEWIS

JOHN Saunders Lewis was an Englishman by birth. He was born in Wallasey in Cheshire on 15th October 1893, the second son of the Reverend Lodwig Lewis, a native of Llanarthne in Carmarthanshire, Minister of the Welsh Calvinistic Methodist Church in Liskeard Road, Wallasey, and his wife Mary Margaret. His education was entirely English. His father gave him some advice as a student and said: 'Look here Saunders, nothing will come of you until you come back to your roots.' His father would not tolerate any English being spoken in the house and Saunders spent the summer holidays with his mother's Welsh-speaking family on a farm in Anglesey. On leaving school, Saunders Lewis went to study English and French at the University of Liverpool. During this time he was inspired to start reading Welsh literature and he was very influenced by the sense of deep Welsh patriotism in a European setting displayed by T. Gwynn Jones who wrote the biography of Emrys ap Iwan in 1912. Even at this time he was very impressed by the Catholic and Latin tradition in Wales before the Protestant Reformation. He was also a great reader of Anglo-Irish literature and was one of the few Welsh people who gave the Easter Rising his support. In 1914, after he had spent a couple of years at Liverpool, the First World War broke out and in his own words: 'As a good English patriot he felt quite happy to volunteer to stop bullying Germany's attack on Belgium'. He joined the South Wales Borderers Regiment as a soldier. After nine months he was promoted to officer which was unusual for the Welsh speaking volunteers were very seldom promoted. On arriving in France with the 12th (3rd Gwent) S W Borderers (Bantam) Battalion he found the French people delightful and, on 14th June 1916, the battalion went into the trenches. He was sent to hospital in Boulogne suffering from trench fever. On return to a new sector (Maroc) he was involved in patrolling and displayed some gallantry in attacking the Seaforth Crater which was recognised by the Brigade staff. During November, the Borderers marched southwards until, in late September, they went into trenches in the Rancourt sector of the Somme. This was the most miserable countryside and the weather was awful; it was very cold and there was a huge amount of mud everywhere. He wrote to his friend and later wife, Margaret Gilchrist, that, 'I can't hope to describe to you the mixture of horror and grotesque humour of this line. Nothing at all of what I have seen before of trench warfare was at all like this. In the line we held we were in shell holes waist high in slime without even the semblance of a trench. Dead men were as common as the living. They had died in all kinds of positions. Numbers had merely drowned. Until your attitude towards them became one of mingled tenderness and sympathy and humorous acceptance one joked with them and often joined them. The Germans began their retirement to the Hindenburg line on 14th March. For three weeks the 12th S W Borderers worked on building railway lines. After this work, the 40th Division, in which they were, came up to the Hindenburg line and were ordered to mount a great assault. Saunders Lewis was wounded in the left thigh and calf; two machine gun bullets went through the knee and a piece of shrapnel blew the calf of his leg away about an hour later. During his time in France he lost his younger brother, Ludwig, but, apart from that, it appears that his war years were not that traumatic for him. He once said they were the best years of his life.

In 1918 he was sent to Athens and served as a personal guard to the Prime Minister where he remained until the end of the war and where he had plenty of time to read and think. He returned to Wales a nationalist. He went on to reject Socialism and believed in a sort of aristocracy immersed in the culture of language who should run Wales. He rejected pacifism and the temperance movement. He had great respect for those who soldiered for their courage and bravery and he himself loved fine food and wine. In 1922 he was appointed head of the department of Welsh at the new University of Wales, Swansea. In a Nonconformist, proletariat and socialist Wales, he was a Catholic elitist and believed in aristocracy. In January 1924, together with two other contemporary Welsh intellectuals, he founded at Penarth a secret society known as 'Y Mudiad Cymrag', the 'Welsh Movement', which became the National Party of Wales. In 1926 he was elected president and he remained in office until 1939. The National Party's aim was dominion status for Wales, self-government under British sovereignty. At the root of Saunders Lewis's politics was a spirituality which certainly governed his attitude towards his country. As far back as 1923 Saunders Lewis had said it would be a great blessing for Wales if some Welshman did something for his nation that would result in his imprisonment. In 1936 the opportunity arose. The Ministry of War was determined to put a training camp and associated aerodrome at Porth Neigwl on the Lleyn Peninsula. Saunders Lewis was against it because he said it would grow and spread. He said it was a holy place and the threat was aimed directly and unfailingly at the heart and life of our language, our literature and our existence as a nation. Some five hundred different organisations protested against the bombing school. Baldwin, the Prime Minister, rejected the protests. About half past one on the morning of Tuesday 8th September 1936 the Rev. Lewis Valentine, D. J. Williams and Saunders Lewis set fire to the sheds, the offices and the building material that the Cowsin company had set up at the PenyBerth site. They walked in to a police station and admitted what they had done. They were arrested and charged with malicious damage. After the first trial was adjourned because the jury failed to agree, a second one was heard at the King's Bench at the Central Court in London. This time a resounding guilty was given by the mainly English jurors. They were sentenced to nine months imprisonment in Wormwood Scrubs.

He found it difficult to get a job after his prison sentence but, in 1941, he published his only volume of poetry, 'Byd y Betws'. He said, 'To the world belongs all materialism and everything sordid and base; to the church belongs everything civilised including the Welsh language tradition.' Two of his poems, 'Mair Fadlyn' and 'Marwnad Syr John Edward Lloyd', are said to be two of the best poems to have been written in Welsh. He was deprived of a lectureship at the University of Wales for a period of fifteen years. In 1952 he applied for a post in the Welsh department at the University of Wales College, Cardiff, and was appointed. He remained there until his retirement in 1957. On 13th February 1962, at the invitation of the BBC, he delivered his hugely important lecture on the fate of the language. He also saw, with current trends continuing, that the Welsh language would die around the start of the 21st century. The lecture had an immediate influence on the younger generation in Wales. They brought a Welsh element to the global protest movement of the 1960s and the Welsh Language Society was founded on 4th August 1962 and, in 1963, Saunders Lewis was its first honorary president. He died on 1st September, 1985 and then it was revealed that, in 1975, Pope Paul V1 had honoured him with the title of

'Knight Commander of the Order of St Gregory the Great'.

There is not a lot to say about his relationships with other men and officers in the trenches but he does say in one letter, 'I shall never forget it. I shall never forget the faces, the stooping backs or the songs that expressed so much men's desires, men's longings and men's grossness, most of them loveable things.' In another letter to Margaret on June 11th 1915 he talks about, 'Being put in charge of the scouts and signalling sections of our battalion. I was sent to instruct them and, as there is a great deal of writing to do in these tasks, I soon discovered that a big proportion of the men is quite illiterate and that to read, write and spell proficiently is quite exceptional so I have set out to form a night school in the battalion.' When it comes to war he talks about, 'The waste of richness and goodness, the vandalism of it all. Even if there were no blood spilt, and no actual ugliness, no positive evil or loss one gains nothing by it.' Saunders Lewis was one of the great Welsh intellectuals of the 20th century. It seems sad that in the South Wales Borderers Museum in Brecon there is little mention of him despite his bravery as a captain in that regiment in the First World War.

Although he was small in stature, he was a man of great style. He was never boring. Unlike his close friend David Jones, he wrote next to nothing about the war and we have very little of what his contemporaries thought of him or he of them but his personality was a dichotomy. He was, at once, a very private person but, at the same time, he became a very public personality. He did not seem to bear any grudge about the class divisions in soldiering or any feeling of being exploited as a soldier. He was, essentially, a man who stood up against bullies but felt himself belonging to something wider than a small nation. He was a European and became a Roman Catholic. He had a wider vision than the introspection of a small nationalist. He made a huge contribution to Wales and its culture and should be recognised for this.

'Saunders Lewis, a Presentation of his Work' by Harri Pritchard Jones
'Saunders Lewis, Selected Poems' translated by Joseph P Clancy
'The Story of Saunders Lewis, the Poet of Welsh Revolution' by Gwynn ap Gwilym

FRANK RICHARDS AND
LLEWELYN WYN GRIFFITHS

FRANK RICHARDS

FRANK Richards, yet another Royal Welch Fusilier, was born in Monmouthshire, orphaned at the age of nine and brought up by his aunt and uncle in the Blaina area of the South Wales valleys. During the 1890s he worked as a coal miner and then joined the Royal Welch Fusiliers in 1901.

He served in India and Burma from 1902 to 1909. In August 1914, he was a reservist soldier who was called up to rejoin the 2nd Battalion the Royal Welch Fusiliers. He saw action in virtually all the major British campaigns on the Western Front without suffering any notable injury. Fifteen years after the close of the Great War, Richards published, in 1933, his classic account of the war from the stand point of the regular soldier; in his case a private, who never rose above that rank in the war but was awarded the Distinguished Combat Medal and the Military Medal. He did not want to move up the ranks as he did not want authority. He was content to do his job as a single man and Robert Graves said he was one of the best in the army. He was present in the front lines when the unofficial truce of 1914 took place and he wrote about it in his book, 'Old Soldiers Never Die'. "We and the Germans met in the middle of no-mans land. Their officers were also out now, our officers exchanged greetings with them. We mucked in all day with them. They were Saxons and some of them could speak English.

By the look of them, their trenches were in as bad a state as our own. It is paradoxical here to quote the words of the Anglican bishop of London in 1915: 'To save the freedom of the world, everyone who loves freedom and honour, everyone who puts principle before ease and life before mere living is banded in a great crusade. We cannot deny it, to kill Germans, to kill them not for the sake of killing but to save the world. To kill the young as well as the old, to kill those who have shown kindness to our wounded, as well as those who crucified the Canadian soldier, who sank the Lusitania and who turned the machine guns on the civilians of Aerschot and Louvin and to kill them, lest civilisation itself be killed.' The last quotation from Frank Richards is about the young Sassoon who Richards said was soon very popular with the men of the company he was posted to. Before this time, he recalled how in the trenches: 'We often had conversations with the enemy and one night one shouted across in excellent English, "Hello 2nd Royal Welch Fusiliers, how are you?" The enemy always seemed to know who was opposite them in the line. In one German regiment they had a wonderful violin player who often played selections from operas and in the summer evenings, when a slight breeze was blowing towards us, we could distinguish every note. We always gave him a clap and shouted for an encore.'

When Sassoon went out on a bombing mission with his soldiers, when he was shot through the top of his shoulder, an old soldier said to Richards: 'God strike me pink, Dick, it would have done your eyes good to have seen young Sassoon in that bombing stunt. He was the best officer I have seen in the line or out since Mr Fletcher, and it's wicked how the good officers get killed or wounded and the rotten ones are left crawling about. If he don't get the Victoria Cross for this stunt I'm a bloody Dutchman. He thoroughly earned it this morning.' Having written his two much acclaimed books, 'Old Soldiers Never Die' and 'Old Soldier Saab', he was interviewed by the BBC for their classic multi-part television documentary 'The Great War' in 1954. He continued to correspond regularly with Robert Graves and died in 1961.

DR LLEWELYN WYN GRIFFITH

DR Llewellyn Wyn Griffith was born on 30th August 1890 in Glanwydden, Conwy. Most of his schooling took place in Blaenau Ffestiniog and Dolgellau. In 1909 he entered the Inland Revenue Department as assistant surveyor of taxes in Liverpool. He enlisted in the Royal Welch Fusiliers in September 1914, was gazetted 2nd Lieutenant in January 1915 and Captained in December 1915. He served in France and Belgium between 1915 and 1919 and was awarded the OBE (Military) and Croix de Guerre.

He wrote, 'Up to Mametz and Beyond' about the great battle involving the Welsh Division. He talked about how, before the division had attempted to capture Mametz Wood, it was known that the undergrowth in it was so dense that it was all but impossible to move through it. Years of neglect had turned the wood into a formidable barrier. Heavy shelling of the southern end had beaten down some of the young growth, but it had also thrown largest trees and branches into a barricade. There were more corpses than men but there were worse sights than corpses. Limbs and mutilated trunks, here and there a detached head forming splashes of red against the green leaves, and, as an advertisement of the horror of our way of life and death and of our crucifixion of youth, one tree held in its branches a leg with its torn flesh hanging down over a spray of leaf. Even now, after all these years, this round ring of man made hell bursts into my vision, elbowing into an infinity of distance the wall of my room, dwarfing into nothingness objects we call real. Blue sky above a band of green trees and a ploughed graveyard in which living men moved worm-like in and out of sight, three men digging a trench, five deep in the red soil digging their own graves as it chanced for a bursting shell turned their shelter into a tomb. Two signallers crouched in a large shell hole waiting for a summons to move but bearing in their patient, and tired inactivity the look of dead men ready to rise at the trump of a last judgement.'

I can only finish with this poem written by Llewelyn Wyn Griffith in 1939:

Faint now in the evening pallor
Answering nothing but old cries
A troop of men shouldering their way
With a new tune I recognise

As something near to Flanders but far
From the dragon years we killed
To no purpose scattered seed
On land none but the devil tilled

That a poet sings as his heart beats
Is no new word but an ancient tale
Grey shadows on the pavement
And Europe sick of its own bale

I have no answer, no rising song
To the young in years who are old
With our arrogance, our failure
Let it be silence, the world is cold

It is vital to recognise that this great regiment, the Royal Welch Fusiliers threw up so many men of poetry and literature, which showed the world something of the great literary tradition of Wales.

AUGUSTUS AND GWEN JOHN

IN 1884 when Gwen John was eight, her mother Augusta died. Gwen had been born in Haverfordwest to Augusta and Edwin, a solicitor, who then wound up his practice and removed his children to Tenby from Haverfordwest. They had not been in Haverfordwest but in Tenby when Augustus, Gwen's brother, was born on 14th January 1878. He was later to become one of the great Bohemians of the early 20th century, an artist of great popularity. The time we are interested in was that of the First World War. He was very keen to be a war artist but the authorities held out against granting permanent exemption from war service and the artist would have to be called up in the normal way. John underwent a number of medical examinations but his legs were not up to war service. There is no doubt he was keen to become a British war artist, but before he was offered that, he had volunteered to work for the Canadian War Memorials Fund, a scheme initiated by Lord Beaverbrook, and he was given an honorary commission in the Overseas Military Forces of Canada. In return, he was supposed to paint a huge picture, between 30-40 feet in length. He wore the uniform of a Canadian major; he set out for war and was billeted on the Somme front at Aubigny. John looked as if he was having a great time. However, he was in his fortieth year and he was subject to deafness. With his rank came a car and a batman and they went out viewing the Vimy front, held by the Canadian Corps.

There were many destroyed churches and he planned to create his picture with tanks, balloons, people and, most important, a crucifix. 'The scene was too beautiful', he told his lover Dorelia, adding, 'I suppose France and the whole of Europe is doomed'. At one stage he almost got into enemy lines by mistake and this was probably the nearest he ever got to fighting.

While on leave he would take advantage of Beaverbrook's hospitality in Paris but, for the most part, he lived in a French chateau. There was a deep melancholy that pursued him at this time and he fell into depression. During this he knocked out one of his fellow officers whom he thought had insulted him. John was rushed out of France by Lord Beaverbrook and the threat of military punishment hung over him. He continued to grapple with the picture but never completed it and there is only one large oil painting called

'The Fraternity' at the Imperial War Museum that reflected his experience in France. His depression was probably caused more by his own feelings about himself than by the devastation on the front. He met his sister Gwen in December 1917 and saw that the change in her was dramatic. Her lover Rodin had died on 17th November. Augustus certainly cheered her up but, after his fight with Captain Wright and the prospect of a court martial, he was not allowed back to France. In the last months of the war, Paris had been subject to artillery bombardment but she had moved out and, eventually, found rooms in the Chateau de Vauxclair near a lonely bay, Pleneúf. When the war was over, Augustus was invited to attend the Peace Conference to undertake the representation of the meeting. He stood out as one of the most flamboyant personalities there and many prime ministers were painted by him and he even painted a portrait of Lawrence of Arabia. The painting now stands in Lawrence's old college, Jesus College, Oxford.

He never really managed to finish the big Canadian war painting nor the Peace Conference painting but he gave eight drawings relating to the war to the Imperial War Museum and also he gave 'Fraternity' to the museum at a very small price. His depression eased at times but there was a fundamental instability which pursued him and he was always a restless spirit.

Gwen had become a Catholic and she found some solace in her religion. However, in 1939 she died in the Hospice de Dieppe aged 63, possibly a greater artist than her brother but she, too, suffered from melancholy and had lived a restless and often dissatisfied life.

The Johns were an extraordinary pair, Augustus more recognised in his own lifetime and one of the leading artists of his day but, later on in the century, Gwen has come into her own and her paintings have been much prized. This talent came from a small Welsh town called Tenby and went on to pervade the capitals of Europe.

'Augustus John' by Michael Holroyd
'Gwen John, Letters and Notebooks' edited by Ceridwen Lloyd-Morgan
'Gwen John, a Life' by Sue Roe

JONAH JONES

HAVING heard his grandfather John talk about Wales, Jonah always believed that the old man had been born there. Jonah was brought up on Tyneside but had a dream of an alternative life, preferably in Wales. He spent some time in Wensleydale, Devon and Kirkudbrightshire, where he did some artistic work, and, although he found life in Wensleydale accommodating, he felt, as a conscientious objector, he had to do something himself about Nazism. He came, gradually, to realise that the war was against a brutal enemy who could not be overcome by peaceful means. He was called up in 1944 to the non-combatant corps and was posted to no 6 Pioneer Corps in Buxton. Various artists befriended him and, on his weekends down in London, he would find refuge in the Central School of Arts. He found army discipline intolerable at times and also the boredom and frustration of the army at home led at least once to his going awol and being punished for it. He was transferred to the Royal Army Medical Corps on 13th November 1944, and started duty for training with 6th Airborne. One of his life-changing experiences was created by his study of Dylan Thomas's 'Reminiscences of Childhood' where he identified with Thomas's growing up in a patch of Wales. By late 1944 he was attending a month's parachute course at the Ringway Parachute School which he found terrifying. There were many remarkable men in 224 Parachute Field Ambulance including James Bramwell, the writer and poet, and John Ryder, who designed books.

Jonah was assigned to the 1st Canadian Parachute Battalion, whose members came from all parts of their homeland with French Canadians forming a quarter. They were lumberjacks, miners and farmers and quite wild. On 2nd January 1945 they arrived in Rochefort. Several days later they moved east to the village of Roy; here they survived attacks from both mortars and Stuka dive bombers. The next big operation was the crossing of the Rhine which took place on 24th March. Later, in 1999, he wrote a two thousand word memoir called, 'The Bloodstone Ring' on this crossing of the Rhine. Jonah made three journeys with the casualties to the MRS, treating and evacuating seven wounded allies and six Germans. Victory came at a cost to the 6th Airborne Division with over a thousand men dead or wounded. Over the next forty days the 6th Airborne Division was at the forefront of a drive of seventy-five miles north east across the North German plain. Jonah was among the first troops to enter Belsen. Nothing would remind him more of the depths of evil in man. When the men saw the near skeletons watching them, many of the soldiers broke down in tears. This was to finish his war. When he thought the war would be finishing and, indeed, it did finish, he found himself again in action, this time in Palestine. Jonah was sent to Jerusalem to organise the library for the army education sector. He did see plenty of action and returned a much wiser man. He had met and befriended a number of artists during his time in the army and, when he came to say farewell to the Canadians when they returned home, he never forgot their toughness, courage and friendship. During a course at Mount Carmel College in Haifa he met another Welshman, Hugh Weldon, who was a major in the 1st Ulster Rifles and had served in the Glider Borne Forces and in the 6th Airborne Division, seeing action in both Normandy (where he won the Military Cross) and Germany, where they became good friends.

Jonah's demobilisation came through in 1947 and he returned to work in Wales including restoring a derelict cottage between Porthmadog and Criccieth. He built fireplaces, plastered walls, hung doors, fixed windows and repaired the roof. Despite his isolation in his cottage, he saw other people including Kyffin Williams, with whom he became friendly. He wanted to earn a living stone-carving and letter-cutting so went to learn at Eric Gill's workshop at Piggots near High Wickham. The six weeks he spent there enabled him to set out on an independent career as an artist and craftsman. He did the lettering for Lloyd George's tomb beside the River Dwyfor near Llanystumdwy. Clough Williams Ellis had designed the tomb and he did the lettering. Jonah's main patron during the 50s was Clough Williams Ellis. The work involved embellishing Portmeirion and many other of his buildings. In between work for Clough, public and private commissions came his way. He was one of the few professional letter writers then practising. Jonah was extraordinarily productive during the 60s. He did much to encourage the flowering of art education in Britain. Later in the 1960s he developed true spiritual fulfilment through belonging to the Catholic Church. He had taken some time to find his religion but his beliefs reflected joy and deep faith. From a literary point of view David Jones's 'In Parenthesis' made a remarkable impression on him and pointed him towards Wales for his life's work. He was a brave man, a talented and creative one who often radiated a spiritual glow.

'Jonah Jones' by Susan Beardmore
'Jonah Jones, an Artist's Life' by Peter Jones

LT. ALUN LEWIS

1915-1944

HE was born in 1915 in Cwmamman near Aberdare, the eldest son of Tom Lewis, a school teacher, who later became a director of education, and of Gladys Evans, the daughter of the Unitarian minister. Although he was brought up in a mining valley which suffered greatly in the Depression, he belonged to a very loving family of three brothers and a sister and, despite his mother's background, Alun never seemed to be overtly religious. In fact, the wonderful holidays they had in Cardiganshire established a deep love of nature and of Wales. He was a man who did not accept convention but had a curious mind and was always questioning. First he went to Cowbridge Grammar School and there the English master, Eric Reed, gave his writing enormous encouragement. He went on a scholarship to the University of Wales, Aberystwyth, when he was 17 and achieved first class honours in History. He then secured a fellowship at Manchester University to read medieval history. After another year at Aberystwyth and a brief period on the local newspaper, he took a teaching post at Lewis School, Pengam. In 1939 he became engaged to Gwenno Ellis who was teaching German at Mountain Ash. She had studied in Germany and gave him some insight into the German and Nazi psyche. Against his will probably, his temperament and some of his principles, he was called up for war service. He spent some time in the Royal Engineers in Longmoor where he wrote a number of poems and short stories. He tried to join the Education Corps but was turned down and went for a commission in the infantry. On 5th July 1941 he married Gwenno at the Gloucester Register Office. After a successful course at the infantry training centre he joined the South Wales Borderers at Woodbridge, Suffolk. The new influx of subalterns found it very difficult to be accepted by the more experienced regular officers and certainly poetry was frowned upon. The work in Suffolk was hard and difficult - improving the defences of aerodromes with barbed wire and fences. There is no doubt he did lack confidence at the start but he took on everything with great enthusiasm and, certainly, one of his fellow officers appreciated how much his men respected him and how much he looked after them. The battalion went on to be stationed at Southend and there his first book of stories was made ready for publication. It was a success. In November 1942 the battalion embarked on a voyage to India where he was put in charge of the ship's education and entertainments. His

Socialist leanings were emphasised on the voyage where he observed the different conditions under which the other ranks lived. At Christmas 1942 the battalion disembarked at Bombay where he had six weeks enforced rest after a clash in a football match. Again, while he was guarding a dam in the Mahartta hills, the culture of India began to impress itself on him. There is no doubt he felt the loneliness that every soldier feels on his first arrival in a new country. One of his most significant poems was 'The Jungle', which evokes the basic Indian scene and experience. In August 1943 he was sent successfully on an intelligence course at Karachi. He returned to his unit as an intelligence officer. His commanding officer was Lt Col Robin Cresswell and his adjutant Alun Gwynne Jones, later Lord Chalfont. The poet entered troubled times as his confidence decreased at the thought of how he would perform as a fighting soldier and he had become friendly with the wife of a British civil servant. In February 1944 the battalion was ordered to Burma. Alun requested permission to go forward and patrol in the forward area. Early the following morning, after hearing a shot his batman found him mortally wounded and he died later that day, Sunday 5th March 1944. A court of enquiry concluded that it was accidental death, although Lord Chalfont stated he believed it was not so, having spoken with Alun the previous night. It was a great talent lost at an early age. He was one of the great poets of the Second World War although he did not see any real action. Like many of the poets of the Second World War, he lacked some of the romantic illusions of the First World War poets. So much was fragmented and so much was mechanical warfare, machine against machine. Men like Lewis did not rush to join the army but were conscripted. Robert Graves speaks about his poetic integrity and so much of his poetry and prose was dominated by the clash of culture and by the disparity between classes. He was a man of great sensitivity and, like so many sensitive soldiers, was always worried that his courage would fail him in the ultimate battle.

The remorselessness and dryness and, in some ways, hopelessness of India affected him. In his heart he always loved Wales. He was popular with his men and many of his fellow young officers. To other older officers with more entrenched views his poetry and writing were an object of suspicion. Here are two of his finest poems:

The Soldier

(Extract)

I within me holding
Turbulence and Time
- Volcanic fires deep beneath the glacier -
Feel the dark cancer in my vitals
Of impotent impatience grope its way
Through daze and dream to throat and fingers
To find its climax of disaster.

The sunlight breaks its flashing wings
Imprisoned in the Hall of Mirrors;
Nightmare rides upon the headlines:
And summer leaves her green reflective woods
To glitter momently on peaks of madness.

But leisurely my fellow soldiers stroll among the trees.
The cheapest dance–song utters all they feel.

The Crucifixion

From the first he would not avoid it.
He knew they would stone and defile him, and looked
*   to it calmly,*
Riding to meet it serenely across the palm leaves, -
Processions in the East being near to bloodshed,
Foreseeing a time when the body and all its injunctions
And life and people and all their persistent demands
Would desist, and they'd leave a policeman
Outside his door or his tomb to keep all in order
While he lay in supremest consummate passion
Passively passionate, suffering suffering only.

And this surrender of self to a greater statement
Has been desired by many more humble than he.
But when it came, was it other than he had imagined?
Breaking his Self up, convulsing his Father in pain?
His will prevented by every throbbing stigma,
The pangs that puffed and strained his stomach wall,
The utter weariness that bowed his head,
Taught him perhaps that more hung on the presence
Of all the natural preoccupations.
Duties, emotions, daily obligations
Affections and responses than he'd guessed.
They'd grown a burden to him, but as a mother
Is burdened by her child's head when her breasts
Are thin and milkless; he knew this awful hanging
Obscene with urine, sagging on a limb,
Was not the End of life, and improved nothing.

'Alun Lewis, Collected Poems' edited by Cary Archard

RAYMOND WILLIAMS

RAYMOND Williams was born to Harry and Gwen Williams on the 31st August 1921 in a rather ugly black stone house near the little villages of Pandy and Crucorney next door to the Offa's Dyke path. His father worked on the railways and had a shift on the signal box. His shifts were twelve hours at a time and 60 or 70 trains came through each day. Williams's novel 'Border Country' is centred on his father whom he described as "full of energy and driven to hard work." His mother Gwen Williams was stern and quiet and a hard task master with him. One of the themes that went through Raymond's life was the idea of community and its association with the Wales he grew up in. Although he lived most of his life in England he saw himself as Welsh European and much of his writing was influenced by Marxism. His 1958 book 'Culture and Society' and the 1961 book 'The Long Revolution' were hailed as a testimonial to the theoretical, historical and critical development of English culture.

His main concentration was on his novels such as 'Border Country' and 'People of the Black Mountains'. He was on the board of a magazine 'The New Left Review' and he was always concerned with the social formation of class which seemed to lie at the centre of contemporary civilisation and was the cause of much discontent. His work and his background were based solidly on the Border Country. After a period at the Pandy Church of England Primary School he succeeded in getting into Abergavenny Grammar School. The great strength of Raymond Williams' kind of Socialism was that it was like the home-grown Socialism of William Morris and some of Raymond's views were coloured by Abergavenny's proximity to the Valleys and the coal mines and the huge battles that went on between the miners and the coal owners and, later, all the issues involved with class warfare. He was so successful at school that he was accepted by Trinity College, Cambridge, one of the great colleges where his Socialism was reinforced by his proximity to the privileged classes. Before the war, while at Cambridge, much of his exertion went into the Socialist Club Bulletin. He was quite happy to join the officer training corps as a man convinced that he had to fight against Fascism. He left Cambridge to fight in the war and, after becoming engaged to Joy Dalling, described as a staunch, pretty, golden-haired woman and the anchor of his life, he started off at the Royal Signals Depot at Prestatyn. He was fit enough to fulfil the army's obsession with physical exercise and was soon designated as officer material.

In January 1942 he was posted to officer cadet school at Larkhill. When asked to register his preference for regimental posting he put down anti-tank regiment first and he joined the 21st Anti-tank Regiment and camped on Salisbury Plain. Even to Williams the make up of the regiment had no clear class divisions in the officers' mess. There was a good mixture including a garage owner, a Maltese refugee, two other students and an insurance agent. On 22nd June 1944, at half past two in the afternoon, the regiment ran ashore on Juno Beach, D Day plus 16. On 28th June the regiment was deployed for action around the hamlet of Putot-Bessin. The fighting was heavy but quite sporadic. Raymond Williams became an acting captain. He said, "How unlike the military history of battles it all was. There was always a dreadful sense of loss."

He was involved in the great battles around Caen. He felt the campaign was one where the men were swept along as in an unforeseeable tide and they were like mere flotsam. At a later stage of his life he perceived the rawness of the Normandy experience could be seen in the wider social experience of the Spanish Civil War and the 1984-85 miners' strike. Raymond carried with him always the unfulfilled duty to fallen comrades. He himself had shown undoubted bravery at Grainville-sur-Odon. His personal diary halts after the Normandy break and it picks up again on 6th September when the Grenadier Group which he was attached to reached Louvlein. After that the troops entered Brussels on 3rd September led by the Welsh Guards. 'Cheering crowds would not let us sleep until 0400 hours. They came back at 0700 hours and started all over again. The tanks by this time were completely covered with flowers.' Afterwards he was involved in Operation Market Garden and they took part in the Guards' armoured dash for Arnhem. The bridge at Nijmegen was taken. They failed to get to Arnhem in time and Q Battery, in which Williams served, was withdrawn in the second week of October for maintenance and rest. Williams was not desperately impressed by many of the Guards officers around him whom he described as 'rather dull.' However, he had proved himself a capable and efficient officer and he was respected and liked by his troops. As regards his wider view of the war, he was always concerned with the suppression of liberated forces in Europe by British arms. He said, 'I only dread being personally involved in it as I would quite definitely face court martial rather than face serving in such circumstances'. Apart from certain vengeful feelings against the Nazis, the power politics of the war's wake

had made him too cynical to want or believe or to work for anything. At the
end of the war he was a very successful editor of the regimental newspaper,
'Twenty One'. He said, 'I have heard so many voices raised in mock horror
at my suggestion that the memory of a Fascist soldier should be guarded in
contempt and hate and never reverence.' He said, 'The banners of the Swastika
that waved at Nuremberg carried death, lying, torture and famine to Guernica,
Rotterdam, Rostoff and Coventry.' He went on, 'Three years before the war
I was a Christian pacifist. The Sermon on the Mount was for me the final
embodiment of the Truth. Faced with war, with Fascism, having seen what was
happening to a Europe that was turning to Hitler its other cheek, I found it no
longer satisfied me. I may have been wrong but the only people who attempt to
translate the great principles of the Sermon on the Mount into political belief are
the Christian pacifists. I respect them. The people I don't respect are the sitters
on the fence who claim to accept Christian doctrine yet accepted and supported
the war. If we were willing to kill we are hypocrites or mercenaries; if we are
not willing to hate let us go on hating Fascism which caused this destruction and
go on working for all that is true, all that is noble, all that is human, all that is
opposed to the horror we hated.'

He became, after the war, a famous and well respected Cambridge don. His
writing and lecturing had all the quality of Welsh Nonconformist Chapel. He
saw Cambridge as an alien citadel which was to be overwhelmed by the ideas
of Socialism. He was a man of his time who managed to accept the role of a
successful officer attached to the Guards Armoured Division but, at the same
time, preserved deeply his faith in Socialism and his aversion to the high
citadels of embedded capitalism. He was a Welshman through and through
who encapsulated the Janus-like quality of the borders. He looked towards
the English bastions of academic excellence for preferment although he was
uncomfortable in them and critical of them; but it is probable that, if he had
not been part of them, his voice would not have been heard so widely. As a
remarkable man of great intellect he encapsulated the history of his time, his
ideas generated debate all over the kingdom and, at the same time, he had
showed his mettle and loyalty to freedom by his skill and courage as a British
army officer.

'Raymond Williams' by Fred Inglis
'Raymond Williams, a Warrior's Tale' by Dai Smith

ANTHONY POWELL

ANTHONY Powell was born in London on 21st December, 1905. His father was an army officer. He was sent to Eton but, even before this, he had decided to nail his colours to the Welsh mast. Sometimes in the past Welshmen have tried to hide their ancestry because among the English upper class they have sometimes been looked down on as Wales was a poor and, in some ways, a subject country. The Tudors, in particular, restored the balance of Welsh identity and perhaps, as an old Etonion, Anthony Powell could have hidden his Welsh origins. It has been said that the worst sort of snob is a Welsh snob but, in Powell's case, like so many of the upper class Welsh, he had traced his genealogy and was both delighted and proud of it. He traced it back to the Lord Rhys or Rhys ap Gruffydd, 1132-1197, who, for many years, ruled over the lands of Deheubarth, the south land roughly comprising Cardigan, Carmarthen with parts of Pembroke, Glamorgan and Radnor. He was undefeated but had an alliance with Henry II and is known throughout Welsh history for instituting the first Welsh eisteddfod. He was persuaded by his wife not to become a crusader; however he died of the fatal bubonic plague. He died having been excommunicated after encouraging his sons to chase the Bishop of St David's from his bed wearing only a woollen shirt and drawers. The Bishop had come to censure Rhys who took against him. The Church, after his death, had his son scourged in penance and the remains of the Lord Rhys were also beaten. Powell traced his ancestry through many generations of middle to upper class Welshmen. His mother was a Wells-Dimock and came also from quite a distinguished family. In March 1901 his father was commissioned into the Welch Regiment which had two battalions made up of the old 41st and 69th of Foot. The regiment had not been chosen particularly because of the Welsh connection but because it was considered by an influential cousin as steady and inexpensive. His father was engaged in the early fighting of the First World War in France. Anthony was sent to an eccentric but relatively smart prep school and then on to Eton. His father, meantime, was on the staff of the 25th Division. At Eton he recalled no sense of inferiority because many other boys' parents were richer and grander. He was made to work hard and was at a slight disadvantage because he did not enjoy games, which he found tedious. Goodhearts House of which he was a member was quite arty which Powell found encouraging.

He was found by his peers to be a thoughtful and serious-minded boy with sensible views and high principles. The family lived in parts of London that were quite fashionable when his father was working at the War Office. He was involved in the setting up of the Eton Society of Arts. There is no doubt that Eton had a certain romantic mystique about it with visions of honour and success and sacrifice which it tried to inculcate into its pupils. Powell left Eton at the end of the summer half in 1923 and he was ready to go. He had enjoyed the house library and had a feeling for literature and books. He came ninth in the end of year July examinations at Eton and was accepted by Balliol College, Oxford. After an interesting time at Balliol, in 1934 he married Lady Violet Packenham, third daughter of the 5th Earl of Longford. In 1939 the next big event in his life occurred when he was asked whether he wanted to be called up for war service. He was very keen and at the interview said his father was a regular officer in the Welch. He was told he could easily get into a funny regiment like that. He believed it was a distinguished regiment with a great roll of battle honours and a tremendous record at winning the army rugby cup. Wellington himself had been an officer in one of its parent regiments, the 69th, which had served as marines on Nelson's flagship at the Battle of St Vincent. He joined the 5th Welch whose commanding officer was a solicitor. Most of the other officers came from banks and lived near Cardiff. The other ranks were from the Welsh valleys and a lot of relations served in the regiment. He was greeted with great hospitality when he arrived at Haverfordwest as befitting a Welsh regiment. In 1831 the 41st was stationed at Arni near Madras with Colonel Sir Edward Williams in command. A letter was sent by the commander-in-chief to say that His Majesty had been greatly pleased to approve of the regiment's being styled the 41st or the Welsh Regiment of Infantry. Until the raising of the Welsh Guards in 1915, no other regiment of the regular army bore a Welsh motto. In the adjutant's letter of 1831 the regiment was described as the Welch Regiment; however one fact is indisputable - in all issues of the army list down to 1920 the 'S' spelling appears. The motto, 'Gwell angau na chywilydd' is interpreted as 'Rather death than dishonour'. The motto had also been borne for many years by the Royal Glamorgan Light Infantry Militia and may well have been adopted by them. In 1831 the regular army included, besides the English regiments, fifteen Scottish and seven Irish but only one represented Wales, the 23rd or the Royal Welch Fusiliers. It was thought the advent of the Welsh Regiment would do a little more justice to the Principality in the army list titles. In addition to its other battle honours, some of the units previously connected with the Welch regiment carried the Honour of Fishguard when the French invaded the town in 1797. They were also the first British guard in the Holy City after the Turkish surrender of Jerusalem. In addition to these interesting battle honours, the Welch Regiment was one of the critical factors in stopping the attempted invasion of Canada in 1813 when it was granted the Battle Honour Detroit.

Powell described his South Walian soldiers as "talkative, good natured, witty, given to sudden bursts of rage, unambitious and delighted by ironic situations".

He said they required a much more flexible approach than English troops, who often lacked the passion of the Welsh. He also thought that Welsh officers were closer temperamentally to their own men and could understand them better. The Welsh, like all Celts, seemed to adhere to different forms of social hierarchy. There were good relations between the officers and men whom Powell described as the "Free tribesmen of British society". The Irish were often very well assimilated into Welsh regiments and often the soldiers were called by the last three figures of their numbers as so many surnames were similar. Welsh officers, when joking or arguing with one another, often used the sort of stage Welsh that could be associated with the Shakespearean character, Fluellen.

Powell, obviously being recognised as a Balliol man, did not spend long in the Welch Regiment and was soon sent on a politico-military course as preparation for being called into Intelligence. He went on to work in the Cabinet Office, liaising with Czechoslovakia and Belgium. After the war, Powell was determined to publish a round of sequel novels. He took some time over the title, but he was captivated by a Poussin painting in the Wallace Collection, 'A Dance to the Music of Time'. He felt the painting expressed through the image of time, thoughts of mortality, of human beings facing outwards like the seasons, moving hand in hand in intricate measure: stepping slowly, methodically, sometimes a trifle awkwardly, in evolutions that take recognisable shape: of breaking into seemingly meaningless gyrations while partners disappear only to reappear, once more giving pattern to the spectacle: unable to control the melody, unable, perhaps, to control the dance. Powell found the figure of time extremely sinister. He opted for a narrator; Nick Jenkins has since been said to be more of an observer than a participant. There was much people said was similar between Powell and the narrator Jenkins and the life the former had experienced with all his interesting connections and artistic friends gave rise to a fascinating set of stories on the activities of human beings. Powell loved gossip and this was reflected in his creation. In Powell's book Jenkins often perceives life as a vast, heaving universe and Powell himself often talks about the absolute lack of interest human beings do in fact feel for each other in daily life. Perhaps there is some nihilism there; however Powell is always interested in people and their goings-on which is reflected in the series of novels which are so much of his own time.

Powell outlasted the century, dying in the early hours of 28th March, 2000, aged 94. The funeral was a traditional understated service very much in his own style. He was always judgmental and spoke out when people displeased him. Going back to our previous observation, I note that it is often said that the biggest snobs of all are Welsh snobs and maybe he had a tendency towards this, but he was immensely proud of his Welsh roots which seemed to give him the Celtic identity which a creative writer of his sort could embrace. There is no evidence that he was an intensely spiritual man but he was aware of the soul of human beings and sometimes full of irony over their actions. He was a stayer who pursued his trade with long term concentration. Ironically, he thought he was a poor man who made good, which sounds amusing coming from an old Etonian schoolboy and Balliol student. He was a man of many parts who deserves to be in the pantheon of writers of the 20th century and an interesting officer of the Welch Regiment.

'A Dance to the Music of Time' by Anthony Powell
'Anthony Powell, a Life' by Michael Barber

REX WHISTLER

REX Whistler was born in 1911 to a middle-class family with no great social ambition. Even at preparatory school, though, he was already beginning to draw. His was an unending flow of funny drawings which made him popular among the boys at prep school. He entered Hailybury in January 1919 and continued to draw. Although he was hardly an intellectual, his brother said of him that he was one of the most sensitively cultured and intelligent young men he had ever met. His artistic appreciation began with a love of poetry including Edgar Allen Poe and Walter de la Mare. At school he was a reasonable rugby player so he was never afraid of physical exercise. He became a student at the Royal Academy School but found that place uninspiring so went to the rival institution, The Slade, where he showed great promise and was a thorough and conscientious worker. While there, he discovered the masters of the 17th and 18th centuries. He was enchanted by the paintings of Poussain, Claude, Watteau and Canaletto. His art appreciation was therefore classical but in poetry he was a Romantic. He was a great scribbler of comments in books and went on to illustrate many of these. One of his great delights was to visit Rome, where he took much inspiration from the wonderful architecture and this classical touch he took into his illustrations. In the 1930's he made contributions to sumptuous limited editions like the magnificent 'Gulliver's Travels' in two volumes published by the Cresset Press in 1930. This was full of large plates, head pieces and tail pieces that were some of his finest work. To appreciate him as an artist was to get beyond the trivialities - advertisements, posters, magazine covers and sets for reviews. There are about twenty books that principally carry his decorations but other achievements include paintings and drawings, murals, landscapes, theatrical scenery, costumes and programmes, a royal box, an Axminster carpet and even a wedding cake. The two probably most important murals he did were, firstly, at the Marquis of Anglesey's great house at Plas Newydd on the island, and, also, the one in the dining room at the Tate Gallery. Both are worth thoughtful and long observation to appreciate their beauty. He became a master in several disciplines such as book illustrations, mural painting, theatre and ballet designs.

When war broke out in September 1939 he applied for an emergency commission in the army. He could well have been appointed a war artist but was quite determined to see action. He was unsuccessful in trying to join the Grenadier Guards but Lt. Col. R.E. K. Letham at the regimental headquarters of the Welsh Guards took a liking to him and gave the regiment a number of distinguished recruits including three Oxford professors, two world famous artists, a brilliant Welsh author, a well known film actor and a prominent race horse trainer. His commission into the Welsh Guards was dated 17th May 1940. He was posted straight into the training battalion which was stationed at Colchester. He only just caught the train and literally fell into the carriage with his uniform and kit in disarray, much to the amusement of the watching soldiers. From 23 February to 7th July 1941 he was posted to the Guards depot at Caterham which was a relatively quiet existence allowing him to paint.

He was offered the opportunity to work on camouflage designs and it was suggested that, because of his value as an artist, he should not risk battle. He said, "If you try to stop me, I shall kill myself" when this was suggested. At the end of May, 1941 the Guards Armoured Division was formed. Rex was part of this and became a tank troop commander He was in some ways a slightly disorganised soldier who was whimsical, very sensitive but very popular. Rex continued to draw including sketches of Welsh guardsmen. Much training went on before the move to France and Rex was very good at building successful relationships with his NCOs and batmen. He was well liked and competent as an officer. On 29th June 1944, twelve days after D Day, the convoy crossed to France. When the tanks advanced George Dolphin, his driver, considered it unlucky that, in addition to the specially made metal box welded to the rear of Olympus, his tank, which carried the artist's small paints and canvases, there were also twenty white crosses. The only reminiscence that his fellow officers had of Whistler doing any artistic work shortly before his death was on Sunday 16th July, their last evening before going into action. Several officers dined at an old fashioned hotel in Bayeaux. They passed a tiny ruined sanctuary where they prayed and, on an area of white wall with a stick of charcoal, Rex drew a Madonna and child. At one point in the following day's attack, the squadron were halted just across the railway line running out of Cannes. Rex's troop on the right flank was left out in the open; two of his tanks crossed the railway line but the wheels of his own tank became entangled in trailing telegraph wires and his tank became stuck. He ordered his guardsmen to get out of the tank while the wire was cut away from its tracks. Suddenly, they came under small arms fire which came from a nearby German position which effectively prevented them from climbing back into the tank. They could not radio Sergeant Sherlock for help and Rex decided to run the distance himself, some sixty yards. He contacted Sherlock but, as he jumped down from his sergeant's tank to run back to Olympus, a mortar blast killed him outright throwing him into the air. He was commemorated by Lt. Col. Windsor Lewis as a fellow soldier who said, "He brought all his talents into play for this new life of his, quickness of decision, imagination, and a vital enthusiasm whilst the sketches he did for us will remain an everlasting joy and memory. He was beloved by officers and men alike. There were no affectations or poses about Rex. He possessed a rich sense of the ridiculous, a strong sense of duty and his character was simple and clean. He was one of the most delightful men the Welsh Guards carried on its roll and he died a hero." He was sensitive, emotional and affectionate and, according to Daphne Fielding, seemed to take his military duties far more seriously than her other friends. He would devote hours to preparing regimental training schemes, studying maps and making notes. His own troop, another officer said, absolutely adored him as well they might for he was in real truth a leader and a guide to them. Lady Cynthia Asquith said, "What I suppose struck me more than anything else about Rex was his extraordinary sensitiveness – his intense awareness. Then, as at the end of his life, he had the easy effortless charm of one who has always been much loved and to whom success had come early and without strain."

'The Laughter and the Urn, the Life of Rex Whistler' by Laurence Whistler
'Rex Whistler's War 1939 – 1944 Artist into Tank Commander' by Jenny Spencer – Smith

DAVID RAIKES

THE Raikes family have lived in Breconshire for many years. They are descended from Robert Raikes who founded Sunday schools. I believe originally they were a Yorkshire family and the Raikes that came to Breconshire, another Robert Raikes a banker, came to work with the de Wintons, built his house Treberfydd in Breconshire near to Llangorse Lake where he also built a church and a school. David was born at Bletchingley, Surrey on 3rd June, 1924; but he always felt his roots were at Treberfydd. He wrote of, 'Wonderful Welsh hills, so gentle and friendly with soft hummocky grass and springy heather, watered by ice cold clear mountain streams springing magically from the ground through soggy moss, tinkling like fairy bells over stones and heather, most magical music. How I love you and always did. And the world has taught me this, that for me there is no greater happiness and it can give no greater pleasure than to live peacefully here among the mountains with water near me and farms about me and the eternal beauty of the hills, and with men and women and their families to share it.' The Raikes were a very distinguished military family and Admiral Sir Iwan Raikes the author remembers well and also the times he, the author, enjoyed at Treberfydd on an autumn's evening playing racing demon with the whole Raikes family including Major General Sir Geoffrey Raikes. In those days that valley, including the valley around Cathedine leading down to Llangorse Lake, was full of joy. Admiral Sir Dimmock Watson and his large family in Trebinchin House, which the poet Sir Christopher Fry used to own, were also a family of fun and the author's father, the Reverend George Rex Morgan, used to enjoy going up to the Admiral's crow's nest at the top of the house where few were privileged to be invited. The Blackhams of Trehalford were also friends of the author and they had bought their house from Dr Cresswell, the much lauded GP who practised in Dowlais, Merthyr. The Raikes were not only a military family but also philanthropic in Breconshire. They went to school at that great English public school Radley College where the author's uncle the great Welsh sportsman Guy Morgan, captain of Wales at rugby and Glamorgan at cricket, taught and battled with the terrible physical sickness of rheumatoid arthritis, a tragedy for such a great sportsman. David, after Radley, did a university short course at Trinity College, Oxford, as an air cadet. He studied Philosophy which had him able to have a look at the new world through philosophical lenses making it a wonderful, mystical, intangible thing. He discovered Dickens in which he found the perfect expression of the interaction of character and environment embodied by the Industrial Revolution.

In April 1943 David Raikes joined his preliminary training unit in London. He felt himself suddenly gripped with horror with the military machine which had utter control over him. He felt like a caged animal as it dawned on him what the loss of freedom would mean. Not only was there the loss of freedom but the loss of individuality. Nevertheless he learned to laugh. He was ordered to Rhodesia for training as a pilot. After nine months in South Rhodesia at Kulmao he became a proficient pilot. His thoughts continually returned to English and Welsh scenes, especially those he loved, particularly the rivers Thames and Wye. He heard the news from Britain of the invasion of France in 1944 and this made him more than ever conscious of the evil of war. He yearned for, 'The day when we shall see the world as one great entity upon which all men walk in freedom and work in harmony, for something more than a nation or a state, for the common good and the common man'. Even in the war he saw divine purpose. 'The purpose is the evolution of man and only man can achieve it. And Christ's agony on the cross was glorious of all, so is man's daily agony in the world. In the end it will be seen that what has been suffered in this world has not been suffered in vain. 'He was sent back to fight and in December David and his crew reached Italy. On New Year's Eve the crew joined the squadron at Falconara, North of Ancona. While he was convalescing, he had an attack of jaundice and, while there, he studied the Fleming report which had been produced on working conditions in Britain. His short experience had left him in no doubt about the central problem. 'In Rhodesia, in New Zealand and America, countries which are still relatively young and still expanding, when a man reaches his teens, he begins to look around for ideas. There are many ways of making money quickly. Life abounds with possibilities; everyone is a budding capitalist. In Britain there was a deplorable sameness which you can sense in the poorer districts; you know that, no sooner is a child born, than he is condemned to the same conditions of living and working, the same fears, the narrow world.' On April 21st, less than two weeks before VE Day, David took off to attack a target in support of the ground troops of the 8th Army. He did not return and no message of any sort was received from his plane. He died with a strong confidence in his fellow men and an equally strong desire to work for an environment which would allow the good that was in them to grow and spread. In his poem, 'Laugh, he have said' it parodied Wilfred Owen, 'Strange friend I said, here is no cause to mourn, none said the other save the undone years, the hopelessness. David's poem reads, 'Laugh he have said, how can I laugh who have known life for something great. Life's but a superficial state, shallow and void you said, Life it is something worth the living and a gift that's worth the giving.' Yes I thought it worth the giving so I gave it and I am dead. I have loved life too well, not for what it gave me, not for life, as the stage for my own display, not for love of living. No, but inspired by the joy of living, the hope of giving, what I could do to life. I looked at life and I heard the song of the desolate hope that lived too long and the men who preached that right was wrong and the cloud of a chaos that hung too long. Over the graves of the dead and all men cried, too long, too long. Have we waited and struggled too long to end a wrong that was not ours and hate is strong.'

'Now Comes the Dawn'
Now comes the dawn, more warily than sleep
More silent than the winds; a little light,
A lifting of the darkness from the night,
A gentle fading of the stars that keep
Their distant watch; a glimmer and a glow,
As though a match had touched some hidden fire,
And, burning with the beauty of desire,
It grows and spreads and brighter yet must grow.

No breath of wind to stir the morning chill,
And long, low banks of cloud most silent lie,
Pale strands of cloud against a paler sky,

And grass and woodland wait, expectant still.

Out of a troubled dream I woke, and stepped
Into a sudden peace. I could but stand,
As though the earth had touched me by the hand,
And said 'Be Still'. For still the valleys slept.

I saw the mountains by the silent lake
Rise like great shadows from another world
Above the mist that in the valleys curled
And hung like waves for ever poised to break.
Dark shapes of hills! White, drifting morning mist.

'Let it be Hushed'

Let it be hushed; let the deep ocean close
Upon these dead. Others may laud their parts,
Raise monuments of marble in their names.

~~~~~~~~~

We grieve not now. There was a time for tears,
When death stood by us, and we dared not weep.
Let the seas close above them, and the dissolving deep.

The Raikes's have made an astounding contribution to Wales and to Great Britain, They deserve a place in this book and no better than it should go to David, one who was a poet and sacrificed his life for our country. He has recently been given a proper burial in Italy.

'David Raikes, Poet' by Charles Wrinch

DYLAN THOMAS

MANY people would disagree with including Dylan Thomas as a war poet. However he was one of Wales's principal poets at the time of the inter war years and the Second World War and going on to the Korean war. And, although many ex-soldiers would confront him as a shirker and a skiver, much of his poetry about the war was serious and impressive. His attitude to war and to military service was a complicated mixture of pacifism, compassion and some guilt. He wrote some poetry about the Great War and, although he found its brutality hideous, he believed that some of the writing and poetry that came out of it was beautiful and glorious. He hated Fascism and some of his poetry was based on the Fascist cruelty of the Spanish Civil War. His book of twenty five poems was published in 1936. He was obsessed with the war to end all wars and one of the main motives in one of these poems was, 'And death shall have no dominion'. He seemed in his poetry to lose hope of resurrection and death was surrounded by a final darkness. In the poems and stories of 'The Map of Love' he talked much about Spain. His point of view was, for the most part, secular and Socialist, denigrating the part the Spanish Catholic Church played in Franco's Spain. In 1939, the Spanish Civil War having ended, the idea of conscription was in the air. He was terrified by the thought and horror of being in a war. He tried to pull many strings in order to obtain a reserved occupation. He went to an army medical board at Llandeilo and his wife Caitlin afterwards insisted that he smoked and drank so much during the previous twenty four hours that the doctors believed he was permanently unfit for duty and gave him a C3 grade which meant that, although he was deemed capable of military service, he would be one of the last to be called up. Between 1939 and 1941 he completed eleven poems and was hired as a script writer for Strand Films to make general documentaries and propaganda films. Meantime, he often picked fights and boasted of his avoidance of the draft and sometimes was beaten up for his views. His film work made sure he was in London for much of the Blitz; he was very frightened by the bombing. 'Among those killed in the dawn raid was a man aged a hundred' was one of his strangest war poems. The man's death was not caused by war but by natural causes which emphasised in a way that nature was even greater than war. In March 1945 he himself came under fire in the unlikely situation of a bungalow near Newquay where he was fired upon without injury by a drunken commando captain called Killick.

One of his great friends, Vernon Watkins, said there was a great difference in Dylan before and after the war. It seemed to have disillusioned him and diminished his great curiosity and enjoyment of life. Certainly, the death camps and their revelation and Hiroshima and Nagasaki gave rise to much of the horror. Thomas often still harked back to the Great War. In one radio programme he talked about Wilfred Owen. 'It is a miracle that in his short and warring life, in the dirt, the blood, the despair, the scarcely tolerable cold, the fire and gas and death of France, he contrived to achieve all of his ambitions and to perfect his original technique'. Dylan Thomas also very much appreciated Edward Thomas of the First World War and Alun Lewis, a Second World War poet. He later went on to talk about the heroic lies and the willingness of the old to sacrifice the young. He was always concerned with the violence and hatred of war; his writing often uses the imagery of war. He wrote once, 'Out of the inevitable conflict of images, inevitable because of the creative, recreative, destructive and contradictory nature of the motivating centre, the womb of war, I try to make that momentary peace which is a poem.' War was at the heart of much of his poetry and, although he saw its terrible negativity, he still could see the small shoots of optimism that sprang from its ending. He had an ambivalent attitude to war; he never wanted to be a soldier and was terrified of war but, at the same time, he appreciated the heroism and bravery that sprang out of it. He was one of Wales's greatest poets and, although his personal behaviour was far from heroic, his poetry reached the heights of inspiration.

'Dylan Thomas, a Farm, Two Mansions and a Bungalow' by David N Thomas
'Dylan Thomas, Poet of his People' by Andrew Sinclair

FUSILIER JOHN OTTEWELL

IN 1944 John was a 19 year old fusilier serving with D Company, the 7th Battalion the Royal Welch Fusiliers, when he landed in Normandy as part of the 53rd Welsh Division. His description of the fighting in which he took part brings alive the reality of war. One of these was fear, the title which he gave to a poem: 'When you're waiting on the start line and the hill is white with smoke, when your rifle butt is clammy and your tonsils start to choke, a little voice keeps pleading as your bowels twist and knot, Oh Mama, mama, quickly fetch my little china pot.'

His poem, *'Evercy' goes: 'Men of the Black Flash, Saucepan and dragon, wading through bayonet wheat, knee high and wet, mortars and 88s playing their overtures, spandaus and schneissers are waiting in set.*

Men of the Black Flash, Saucepan and Dragon limping it back all haggard and pale. 200 dead for a handful of prisoners, just one consolation they've brought up the mail.'

At the same place he wrote: *'The Weeping Elm', 'Poor stark deluded shattered elm with dripping trunk and riven bole, Full many a year you ruled serene, Over the green clothed valley's rustic scene where flowers and bees and head high-fern paid homage to your queenly realm but now caught in the pall of battle, drifting smoke and earth, concussed you bleed in silent withering shame for God made beauty turn to man-made hell and as I gaze across to Calvary Hill on Him transfixed upon his stoned cross still pleading vainly for the love of errant man I render soft sweet orisons for your poor beleagured soul to Heaven above from sodden mud bespattered hole'.*

Another one called, 'On Parade' was written at a British war cemetery: *'I saw an army on parade, rank upon rank immobile, erect in shining armour and in my eyes each soldier carried out the perfect drill. No foot, no rifle but a wry precision, sheer perfection. A sergeant major's dream come true. And having watched this proud display for one long morning on a green clothed hill I left the seat with misted eyes to join my pilgrim friends in local bar, and as the sun came down a lonely bugle played the final requiem for those in splendid shining ranks still waiting for the order to dismiss.'*

John's story tells of the fear, terror, loneliness, excitement, joy, boredom, despair, love, hate, and sheer and utter exhaustion, mental and physical. Rarely does he extoll the glory of war, the hideous business of fellow man killing fellow man in the name of patriotism and democracy, nor is it intended to be interpreted as flag-waving jingoism inspiring future generations of young men to follow the flag into the maelstrom of war in order to prove their manhood. No, it is none of that but just merely condemning the inhumanity of it all and the gross wastage of young lives that can only be justified when it opposes oppression and thwarts and defeats those oppressors who would take from us our sacred freedom and liberty. Such was World War Two. The oppressor, Adolf Hitler, was hell bent on conquering and enslaving the world. In June, 1944, this tiny bastion island was one of the places which stood in his way. If we had gone down then, the entire world would have gone down with us; the Nazi jackboot would have ruled the land and the waves. John went on to serve with the 1st Armoured Division in Northern Italy and Austria. He helped Tito's partisan army and next served in Trieste, Venice and the Adriatic ports.

John has suffered physically and mentally including periodic panic attacks brought on by memories of traumatic wartime experiences. When a signals runner, he was frequently caught out in the open during shell and mortar bombardments which deafened him and blew him off his feet on a number of occasions. He had a pension grant of eight shillings and sixpence for three years terminating in a lump sum of £80. As ever, the British government hardly compensated their troops for the terrible trials they suffered; this still goes on today. John has been a great bastion in Brecon for the Royal Welch Fusiliers and he raised money for a splendid bench in their memory which is located outside Lloyds Bank in the town.

'A Cry From the Heart' by John Ottewell

A WELSH FAMILY IN THE WARS

Jonathan Morgan's story

THE story really begins at Christ College, Brecon, where Jonathan, who was not a great academic, was highly impressed by the whole ambience that the South Wales Borderers brought to the town. Their officers seemed to live in lovely houses and the magnificence of the parades, that were often held in Brecon, left a significant mark on his psyche. His father had been a very brave padre to the 60th Rifles in the Second World War, and it was not until after his father's death that he came to realise how brave he had been. His uncles and great uncles were all in portraits around the school as some of the greatest Welsh rugby players of their generations. His Godfather, Jim Jones, who had been commissioned into the South Wales Borderers, had won an MC in Burma and his grandfather, Major T. L. Morgan, had survived the trenches in the First World War. From an early age, thanks to these influences, Jonathan was determined to join the South Wales Borderers. After a relatively easy run which involved not a huge expenditure of effort, he won a scholarship to the Royal Military Academy, Sandhurst. His first taste of the army was the pre-Sandhurst army outward bound course at Towyn in North Wales. This was an extraordinary course, where future cadets were put in patrols under a regular instructor. At dawn, the participants would have to run down to the sea about two miles away from their huts and take a dip. Rock climbing was an essential ingredient, as was canoeing. Jonathan, at this stage in his life, suffered from mild vertigo, and, although the cadets did not have to lead, he found the experience raw and scary. Again with canoeing, as he came from a town that had no swimming pool, his swimming was rudimentary and he found that whole activity very frightening. The Mallory Patrol to which Jonathan belonged had an amazing instructor who must have been about 6ft 5ins and was called Tiny.

On the expeditions he would continually appear on crests of hills above the patrols, watching how they performed. The greatest test was a sort of orienteering course; the bigger the peak one went up, the more points one got. Each patrol tended to have a weak link who had to be managed so that he could take in as many peaks as physically possible. It was three weeks of the highest possible activity and exercise and, at the end of it all, the potential cadets were ready for Sandhurst.

Sandhurst in 1969 was a shock to any new cadet's constitution. It was not exactly brutal but the first term was designed to break the cadet into leadership. The company intake consisted of about 14 cadets, mostly from the United Kingdom, but some came from all over the world. One was reduced to an absolute basic personality; very little concession was given to school, background or family and, as such, it was quite a fair system. The days were spent under the watchful eye of a guard sergeant who was one's platoon instructor and hours were spent on the drill square and perfecting one's fitness. Also much training was done on the weapons one would have to use in the real army. It was an exhausting and gruelling existence, made worse at the end of the day when one was put in the charge of a cadet government, - senior cadets who supervised all the bulling and cleaning of one's kit. There was no time for oneself and, certainly for the first four or five weeks, one was not able to get away from the Academy. A number of people fell by the wayside and, tragically, there was, at least, one suicide. However, on the positive side, one made lifetime friends within one's platoon and learned an enormous amount about oneself and how far one could go. Jonathan survived this because he was fit, although he found some of the more practical things like weapon training quite difficult. At the same time as all the training, he managed to play for the Academy rugby side. There were six terms altogether, two years in total; three years were academic when one spent a lot of time in the classroom. During these two years there were a number of exhausting exercises including two trips to the Eifel in Germany. Also, during the long summer holiday, in the middle of the two years, Jonathan went off to Muscat in Oman which proved fascinating, as he was attached to the Muscat regiment for six weeks at a time when Sultan Quaboose had just taken over and was showing himself to his people, which was a huge change, as his father had been a recluse.

Everywhere they went, there were huge parties for the new Sultan consisting of thousands of white robed Arabs, many letting off their old fire pieces as they greeted the young Sultan. As Jonathan had been brought up in a quiet country vicarage in Breconshire, the whole episode was a huge culture shock for him and the boundaries of his mind were expanded accordingly. One of the sadnesses of Sandhurst at the time, and of his education at Christ College in Brecon, Wales, was the lack of women and, consequently, the lack of their friendship and softening qualities in a harsh all male military culture. In later life, looking back, Jonathan thought this a huge deficiency.

There is no doubt that passing out of Sandhurst was an achievement. Jonathan never felt, as a Welshman, that he was discriminated against although he was called 'Taffy', but the camaraderie and the feeling that one was in the best military academy in the world did much for all their self-esteem. It was with great pride that they all passed out. Jonathan had not set the Academy on fire, but was a good average cadet who made junior under officer and, as a result, felt a lasting sense of achievement.

In 1971, after two years at Sandhurst, Jonathan joined his regiment The Royal Regiment of Wales in Osnabruck in North Germany. The first night became very significant to him. He arrived in the mess to find two subalterns eating dinner together, obviously not included in the party of junior captains and other subalterns, who were dressed up to the nines in dinner jackets and, therefore, about to go out to dinner. He realised later that these two men had been excluded because they were not considered of the right social type. One was a schoolmaster's son from a comprehensive school in Merthyr and the other a paymaster's son who had been a very successful rugby player at Monmouth School. Gradually, over the next week, it dawned on Jonathan how significant was the amalgamation that had taken place to form the new regiment, The Royal Regiment of Wales, out of the South Wales Borderers and the Welsh Regiment. The former considered themselves a rather smart regiment that had originally been formed in England by Sir Edward Dering in Kent and they prided themselves on the performance of the regiment in the Zulu Wars, especially at Rorke's Drift. Their officers often call themselves the 24th rather than The S.W. Borderers as if the South Wales bit had a slight social stigma attached to it. From what Jonathan saw, they were mostly recruited in the officer's mess from English public schoolboys, who, at times, regarded the Welsh as colonial troops. He obviously could not speak for the S.W. Borderers as a regiment as he had never served in it, but he observed this as the psyche of the officers who had come into the new regiment. The Welsh Regiment, on the other hand, had no such social aspirations and was quite happy to be an ordinary regiment recruited to some extent from the South Wales middle class, but again, Welsh officers were not predominant. In addition, the Borderers had a number of families who had served in that regiment through the generations and he could not see that many of them were Welsh. Subtle infighting went on to establish which culture would take control and, as time went on, Jonathan had no doubt that the S.W. Borderers were in charge. There was also a hint that they had read up on the Marcher lords, and maybe there was a theory that the Welsh were ill-disciplined and, although brave, needed a hard rule, very much dictated by a very rigid hierarchy. The fact that the men were Welsh and many of the officers English certainly undermined Jonathan's own confidence in his Welshness, a trait that was to hound him throughout his short career. One of the things that hit his confidence at this time was being taken out by two sharp young captains and being told that, as a Welshman, he should not expect to get anywhere in the regiment. There was a drinking culture in the mess which did not appeal to Jonathan, but life was made more unpleasant by the fact that, when he went to bed earlier than the rest, he was often turfed out of bed. There was an element of bullying in the culture which did not endear mess life to him.

In the second week, like so many young subalterns in the British Army, he was thrown in at the deep end. He was ordered out on one of the great field training exercises that took place in the Autumn, commanding a combat team of four Leopard tanks, two guided weapons carriers, four scout cars and his own platoon. He was given an axis on which to advance over a couple of days and a hundred miles, acting as enemy to a larger battle group. His most undistinguished moment was on a recce in a helicopter which had to land because he was about to be sick. On landing, an exercise umpire jumped out from behind a hedge and he was officially captured. The exercise took them through the Weser Valley, and included a scary crossing of the river Weser at night in armoured army personnel carriers. The exercise took about three weeks, and the troops seemed to have the freedom of the German countryside. It was exciting and thrilling, however unreal. There was always the threat of a Russian invasion of West Germany but these were definitely war games and it was not until a year later that the real bullets were flying when the regiment was ordered to the Ardoyne in Belfast. Just before the regiment went to Belfast, a recce party went across a couple of weeks beforehand and it was rather paradoxical that, on the recce, a bus full of unarmed officers and NCOs of the regiment went down the Falls Road by mistake, having taken a wrong turn. In April 1972, reality struck home. A Company under the incorrigible Major John Ayres moved in to the former primary school on the Old Park Road. This was close to the notorious Bone area dominated by the IRA, and to the Ardoyne a hugely Catholic area. It was not far from the Shankhill, and the rest of the area was a mixture of working class and middle class homes, and streets belonging to the different tribes. It was four months of undiluted hell for Jonathan. He had hated the sight of blood since his childhood and there were many casualties. He spent one week of three on road blocks with his platoon, during which they had one major incident with gunmen. Patrol week was the worst week, when he led a patrol every other night. The back alleys of the Bone were often covered in dog excrement mixed up with glass, so the soldiers boots could be heard anywhere. There were many gun battles, and it was with great sadness one day that Jonathan saw the body of an eight year old girl being carried up the Old Park Road by one of his veteran corporals after she had been shot running out of the sweet shop and not shot by the army. His most unbrave act was, having hidden behind a wall with one of his corporals, they heard an IRA sniper open up not far on the other side. Jonathan let his corporal look over the wall first. Probably his bravest action was to go after a car containing gunmen that had careered into the Bone and had packed up. He was ordered in with three men to check the car out. His driver said 'Let's pretend that we've been in there'; but they faced up and went in. In the four month tour, casualties were something like six killed for the battalion and 26 injured. This was by far the worst year of the troubles and never again would the deaths of soldiers, terrorists or the incidence of bombings and shootings ever reach these heights. It would witness 1,853 bombings, 10,564 shootings and the deaths of 129 soldiers, 17 R.U.C.

officers, 223 civilians and 98 terrorists. Jonathan was posted out two weeks early, paradoxically to do the platoon commander's course in Warminster. He was near cracking point and it was partly this operation that led to his subsequent post traumatic stress illness. It was an exceedingly tough tour for anyone but for someone who had been brought up in a quiet vicarage in Breconshire, it was particularly traumatic but although he had survived without cracking up, he was on the verge of it. Warminster was another of those hectic army courses where one's feet never touched the ground. But it was a joyride compared with Ireland. He went back out to Germany to take over his platoon again and did another very successful exercise season. However, he never found the battalion a very pleasant place; there was a lot of snobbery, and, when he first joined, he was hardly spoken to for months and was not made welcome. He felt his Welshness a disadvantage, and in the Darwinian competition that was prevalent in the army at the time, any minority was at a disadvantage. He felt that there was only a small number of his contemporaries he could really trust, and no one had even thanked him for being quite brave in Northern Ireland. He was thus delighted when he was offered a posting to the Welsh Brigade depot at Crickhowell for two years.

There was no doubt that Jonathan still had feelings of combat inadequacy, as in some ways he had, in his own view, not been tested sufficiently in Northern Ireland. So, at the depot, he embarked on a number of experiences which set out to test his nerve. The basic ski course in Winterberg was not a great test of nerve nor really was the mountain leader certificate, which he failed on Cader Idris because he was not prepared to trust his own knots going down an abseil. Much bigger tests were the army basic rock climbing course, which was a huge test for Jonathan because he suffered from vertigo and, after a week of what he thought were gruelling climbs, he was a nervous wreck and was not allowed to be trusted with the lead of a climb. This week, in a way, was as scary as the Northern Ireland experience and then he decided to push himself even harder by putting himself on the army yacht hands course. He was scared of the sea and a very poor swimmer, and at one stage the course involved him clinging on to the pulpit, tied on with a karabena going through the race off Weymouth in the middle of the night. Returning from these courses, he broke his ankle playing rugby against the Usk College of Agriculture and then things started to go wrong. He suffered endless sleepless nights and breathing difficulties. At times he even put himself into casualty.

Once he did this whilst crossing London and was told there was nothing wrong with him. He was sent off on holiday/exercise with Major Morgan Llewellyn's Royal Welsh Fusilier Company to Cyprus. Here he took no part in training but spent the whole time going in to see the doctors trying to resolve what was wrong with him. Nowadays, post-traumatic stress would have been diagnosed but then he was just sent empty away. When he returned to the U.K., a shadow of his former self, he fell in love with a beautiful girl but it was an unrequited affair, which added to his ills.

At the same time as all this was happening, he had been taking a fifth A Level at Ebbw Vale Technical College in order to try and reach the required standard for university entry. He began to realise his nerve had gone and the thought of going back to the regiment was quite ghastly. His tutor, Paul Murphy, who later became Secretary of State for Northern Ireland and Wales, was a brilliant teacher and knew his subject, British Government and Politics, backwards. His enthusiasm and knowledge was passed on to Jonathan during that year, and the latter scored an A grade at A Level, putting him in line for sponsorship to his first choice university, Aberystwyth, to read International Politics at its famous department, many of whose lecturers lectured at the Army Staff College. Jonathan, at the age of twenty three, arrived a wreck. It was not helped by starting at the bottom again in an environment which little recognised past experience. However, after a few weeks, he met a beautiful, sympathetic, sensitive girl who nursed him back to health. He made friends with Jim and Frances Evans. Jim was later to become head of British American Intelligence in Washington on September 11th at the time of the destruction of the Twin Towers. Bob Stewart was also a friend, who later commanded the Cheshires in a high profile tour of Bosnia. One of the great joys of Aberystwyth was the rugby league on a Wednesday afternoon when Jonathan got together with Dr Doug Porch, a former Vietnam veteran, and they played together in the centre of one of the student halls. Other great times were the shooting parties, beach parties and the lovely fishing for sewin in the Rhiedol Valley. Also in the long summer holiday he went to the regiment in Berlin where, on one occasion he commanded the soldiers who guarded Hess. His health was restored, but deep in his sub conscious was the threat that he would have to go back to the regiment after three years. This period came to an end and he returned to the regiment, which almost immediately went out to Belize. He had not soldiered properly for five years, his motivation and nerve had gone and he was isolated in a far off country away from his friends among fellow officers who felt he had had an easy time and were not prepared to help. They did not seem to realise that he'd lost his soul, and although he was quickly transported out of airport camp in Belize City, which was like a shoal of piranhas and where he spent some evenings on his own sleeping in the chapel, without any help from any chaplain and no help from his regiment who eventually posted him up country out of the way. He was sent off on a number of trips to try and make him recover, including the shock of being sent to Bermuda to put down the riots. All to no avail. By the time he got back to the U.K. he had almost gone mad, and, eventually, had to persuade the authorities to put him into the main army hospital for psychiatric problems called the Woolwich. His treatment was perfunctory and hardly included any therapy; plenty of pills and he was told a number of times to sort himself out. After two months he was no better and his parents took him out. He was invalided out officially and sent to Barts Hospital which had no room for him, so he was put in for a couple of days in a doss house in Balham.

Luckily, a friend suggested a flat sharing agency and he found himself in a high-class flat in Wandsworth. He had to stay in London, because that was where his therapist from Barts Hospital was. He had little money, so worked for four months in the toy department of Harrods where he rose to the rank of Father Christmas. Then he did agency cleaning, lasting only one day at the Bank of England kitchen where he had left water on the floor and so got the sack. He cleaned up after Arabs in their smart flats, and served as a waiter at drinks parties. London is not a very friendly place for former veterans with post-traumatic stress. He limped on, getting a teaching job at a small independent school in London but finally cracked when he thought he was in the middle of a nuclear war, rushing down the Wandsworth Bridge Road without his trousers. He was rescued from the police by his brother, a lawyer, and sent back to an old psychiatric hospital at Talgarth in the Black Mountains near Brecon. His psyche was disturbed by supernatural struggles and what the Desert Fathers would have called demons. Living in a ward full of unpredictabilities, he finally had a waking dream that he was taken to a high altar by a godfather figure called Bishop Lucy who had haunted the chapel of his old school at Christ College Brecon. He was given communion by a presence he dared not look at, but, from that time on, he started to recover. There was only one more relapse, when on a course at the Marlborough Summer School, and having, read some Siegfried Sassoon, he saw Sassoon's name in the Great Hall and, afterwards, went into the chapel where an effigy of the Virgin Mary took on a ghostly hue and blessed him. He was one of the lucky ones. For all the analysis that therapists might diagnose in his psyche, he believed he had been saved by divine intervention and never looked back. Many veterans have not been so lucky. He now dedicates his life partly to raising money for Combat Stress and to try and make sure others do not have to go through what he went through.

The Morgans, on both sides, were descended from men of religion, and, perhaps when the psyche is deeply traumatized, there is a gene that ignites religious experience. Science has not yet solved this conundrum. Jonathan's poetry was inspired by the sea and countryside of Wales.

THE SEWIN

The night was dark, and the fish swam,
No-one knew from whence they came;
They were big and silver and shy
And were very afraid of man.

The darkness was full of haunting,
The trees of strange shape and sound.
The water shrilled like fairies calling,
And the rocks were like graves flaunting.

Electricity was in the air,
Would the great fish be caught?
Would their death presage
Another nail in the Celtic coffin?

That darkness Vaughan called dazzling
Surrounded the lonely fisherman;
The Western shore was calling,
And the depths were impenetrable.

SCREENS
Screens are made of wood;
They hide the eternal cobweb
Where the spider hunts for food
And traps the flies by stealth

The screen puts up the kites;
Red and black they fly
To fool the unsuspecting heights
With the unknowable clouds

The clouds storm the sky
And frighten the kites,
Who drop to the web
Behind which lies the
Screen's mysterious rood.

THE PEREGRINE

He looks down from the craggy heights
And laughs at creatures of so small a size,
His view is one of most remarkable sight
He sees where everything lies.

The angular beak and curved talons
Strike fear into those of no defence;
Not for him the comfort of roomy salons,
He is certainly of raw presence.

A minute movement affects their eye,
And all is spring and tremor;
He knows where all do lie,
And through his swoop are soon to die.

Like a chieftain of old, he surveys his land
And trains the chicks into his band;
Look out the quarry he espies,
No mercy will he grant their cry.

THE WILD GOOSE

On that lonely estuary, its cry was heard afar;
No comfort sound was this, but eerie like a star.
It came from further reaches where no man had been before;
It echoed across the mudflats and was a cry of raw.

Freedom its bugle sounded from above the sea;
It commanded here all that was right and free.
It did not desert its comrades whenever they did fall,
It hallowed friendship first, more above all.

THE DEMONS OF THE NIGHT

The demons of the night
Surround the basking bed,
No rest will they allow
The mind and other sights;

Water may allay the disturbance,
But back to bed again regenerates it;
All is not completely lost,
Because behind all is the Presence and its Comfort

Restless heart, restless spirit,
Whereto yonder will you travel alone?
The shadow has been cast,
And it must be stood up to without reserve.

THE LADY OF ICE

The mountains rule
Mysterious and wild,
Roots go in deep
And earth drips with webs.

The twilight dreams,
And romance is dulled
With menace and the dark,
All is covered in mist.

The lady beckons,
But all is in vain;
Her mind is treacherous
And cooled by ice.

The future may be bleak,
But promise must never be lost;
The Lord rides high
In the castle of the spirit.

There is no doubt that Jonathan's recovery was partly attributed to the effect that his surroundings in nature, based on the beautiful Brecon Beacons and the lovely River Usk, the Black Mountains and the Wye Valley, Mynydd Epynt and, in particular, that lovely common Mynydd Illytd, just above Brecon, were deeply impressed on him. Nature has its own healing and that, coupled with a sacred sense of God's creation, helped him to recover his sanity whilst surrounded by the generosity of his childhood friends.

Many veterans do not have this support or a beautiful area in which to live. They languish in poor accommodation and an environment which makes no contribution to recovery. Because so many of them are broken in spirit and will take years to recover, if ever; they need to be looked after financially so that they can enjoy the quality of life they deserve, having put their lives on the line for this country. This is still not happening.

In addition, alternative therapies should be used to help soldiers suffering from mental illness. Jonathan Morgan found great balm for his spirit from music. Maybe it was because he was Welsh, but it is generally proven that music has great healing qualities and so he hopes that these are all available for the injured veterans it is, however, very difficult to get information out of the system and to put back in what has worked with many individuals, especially when confronted with the scientific reductionism of many professional psychiatrists.

Jonathan Morgan was educated at Christ College, Brecon, R.M.A. Sandhurst, and Aberystwyth, Cardiff and Glamorgan Universities. He also taught at U.W.I.C. (now Cardiff Metropolitan) for nine years. Jonathan's father, the Rev. G. Rex Morgan, Chaplain to the King's Royal Rifle Corps and Senior Housemaster at Christ College, Brecon, was a well-known prisoner-of-war. It is interesting that Christ College former pupils won 23 MCs in the first World War.

Jonathan's was a great Welsh sporting family which included Guy Morgan, Captain of Cambridge University and Wales at rugby and Glamorgan at Cricket, and Dr. Teddy Morgan, Captain of Wales and the British Lions at rugby. Rex's cousin Guy (not the rugby player), was a Royal Navy Lieutenant and prisoner-of-war who wrote the well-know play 'Albert R.N.' Jonathan's mother, Glenys, was the daughter of Morgan T.L.Morgan, Adjutant of the 15th Welsh in the early part of the Great War.

As well as a sportsman himself Jonathan is a 3rd Order Anglican Franciscan. He was invalided out of the Army with PTSD or related illness in 1980 and had served with the Royal Regiment of Wales as a Captain which included an horrific tour of Northern Ireland in the Ardoyne and Bone districts of Belfast.

. . . . . .

Robert Macdonald, an artist who lives near Brecon, is a past chair of the Welsh Group, the senior association of professional artists in Wales, and first elected chair of the Royal Watercolour Society of Wales. He is a graduate of the Royal College of Art. His childhood was shaped by the Second World War - in 1942 at the age of seven his family home was destroyed in a German bombing raid and he spent the rest of the war as an evacuee in Somerset.

ISBN 978-0-9930268-0-5

PRICE: £10

9 780993 026805